MW00508991

THEOSOPHICAL

MANUALS

XV

THEOSOPHY THE MOTHER

OF RELIGIONS

The Aryan Theosophical Press
Point Loma, California
1907

THEOSOPHICAL MANUALS

XV

THEOSOPHY: THE MOTHER OF RELIGIONS

BY

A STUDENT

The Aryan Theosophical Press
Point Loma, California
1907

COPYRIGHT, 1907, BY KATHERINE TINGLEY

PREFACE

THE remarks under this head are intended to be introductory to each of the Manuals.

First, as to the spirit in which they are offered. These manuals are not written in a controversial spirit, nor as an addition to the stock of theories awaiting public approval. The writers have no time to waste in arguing with people who do not wish to be convinced, or who ridicule everything which is new to their limited outlook. Their message is for those who desire to know — those who are seeking for something that will solve their doubts and remove their difficulties. For such, all that is needed is a clear exposition of the Theosophical teachings; for they will judge of the truth of a teaching by its power to answer the questions they ask. People realize, much more now than in the early days of the Theosophical Society, the value of Theosophy;

for the ever-increasing difficulties engendered by selfishness and materialism, by doubt and the multiplicity of theories, have created an urgent demand which it alone can satisfy.

Again, it is necessary to state clearly and emphatically the genuine teachings of Theosophy, as given by the Founder of the Theosophical Society, H. P. Blavatsky, and her successors, William Q. Judge and Katherine Tingley. For, as H. P. Blavatsky predicted, there are persons who have sought to pervert these teachings and turn them into a source of profit to themselves and their own selfish and ambitious schemes. The true teachings do not lend themselves to such purposes; their ideals are of the purest and most unselfish. Hence these persons have sought to promulgate under the name of Theosophy a perverted form of the teachings, from which Brotherliness and other pure motives are omitted, and which contains doctrines which H. P. Blavatsky showed to be maleficent and destructive. As these pseudo-Theosophists have gained a certain amount of notoriety by using the names of the Theosophical Society and its Leaders, it is necessary to warn the public against them

and their misrepresentations. Their teachings
can easily be shown, by comparison, to be directly contrary to those of H. P. Blavatsky,
whom they nevertheless profess to follow. Instead of having for their basis self-sacrifice,
self-purification and the elevation of the human
race, these teachings too often pander to ambition, vanity and curiosity. In many cases
they are altogether ridiculous, and only calculated to make people laugh. Nevertheless,
as these travesties have served to discredit the
name of Theosophy and to keep earnest inquirers away from the truth, it is well that the
public should know their nature and origin.
They are the work of people who were at one
time members of the Theosophical Society,
but who did not find in it that food for their
own personalities of which they were really in
search. So they turned against their teachers
in wounded pride and vanity, and started little
societies of their own — with themselves at
the head.

The writers of these Manuals have no personal grievance against any such calumniators.
Inspired by a profound love of the sublime
teachings of Theosophy, they have made it

their life-work to bring the benefits which they have thereby received within the reach of as many people as possible. And they feel that they will have the hearty sympathy and co-operation of the public in exposing folly and bringing the truth to light.

Theosophy strikes unfamiliar ground in modern civilization, because it does not come under any particular one of the familiar headings of Religion, Science, Philosophy, etc., into which our age has divided its speculative activities. It dates back to a period in the history of mankind when such distinctions did not exist, but there was one Gnosis or Knowledge embracing all. Religion and Science, as we have them today, are but imperfect growths springing from the remnants of that great ancient system, the Wisdom-Religion, which included all that we now know as religion and science, and much more. Hence Theosophy will not appeal to the same motives as religion and science. It will not offer any cheap and easy salvation or put a premium upon mental inactivity and spiritual selfishness. Neither can it accomodate itself to the rules laid down by various schools of modern thought as to

what constitutes proof and what does not. But it can and does appeal to the Reason. The truth of doctrines such as Theosophy maintains, can only be estimated by their ability to solve problems and by their harmony with other truths which we know to be true. But in addition to this we have the testimony of the ages, which has been too long neglected by modern scholarship, but which is now being revealed by archaeologists and scholars, as H. P. Blavatsky prophesied that it would in this century.

It may perhaps be as well also to remind those who would criticise, that the state of modern opinion is scarcely such as to warrant anybody in assuming the attitude of a judge. It would be quite proper for a Theosophist, instead of answering questions or attempting to give proofs, to demand that his questioners should first state their own case, and to be himself the questioner. The result would certainly show that Theosophy, to say the very least, stands on an equal footing with any other view, since there is no certain knowledge, no satisfying explanation, to be found anywhere.

Since the days when the wave of materialism swept over the world, obliterating the
traces of the ancient Wisdom-Religion and
replacing it by theological dogmatism our religions have had nothing to offer us in the way
of a philosophical explanation of the laws of
Being as revealed in Man and in Nature.
Instead we have only had bare statements
and dogmatic assertions. The higher nature
of man is represented by such vague words
as Spirit and Soul, which have little or no
meaning for the majority. The laws of the
universe are briefly summed up under the
term " God," and all further consideration of
them shut off. Then came a reaction against
the dogmatism of religion, and man pinned
his faith to knowledge gained by study and
reflection, limiting his researches however to
the outer world as presented by the senses,
and fearing to trench upon the ground which
dogmatic theology had rendered the field of
so much contention. The result of this has
been that neither in religions nor sciences,
have we any teaching about the higher nature of man or the deeper mysteries of the
universe. This is a field which is left entirely

unexplored, or is at best the subject of tentative and unguided conjectures.

Until, therefore, religious teachers have something definite, consistent, and satisfactory to offer, and until science can give us something better than mere confessions of nescience or impudent denials with regard to everything beyond its own domain, Theosophy can afford to assume the rôle of questioner rather than that of questioned, and does not *owe* anybody any explanations whatever. It is sufficient to state its tenets and let them vindicate themselves by their greater reasonableness; and any further explanation that may be offered is offered rather from goodwill than from any obligation.

Theosophy undertakes to explain that which other systems leave unexplained, and is, on its own special ground, without a competitor. It can issue a challenge to theology, science, and other modern systems, to surpass it in giving a rational explanation of the facts of life.

Again, there are some questions which it is beyond the reach of the human mind, in *its present stage of development*, to answer;

and it would scarcely be just to arraign Theosophy for not answering these.

Judgment should in all cases be preceded by careful study. There are always those who will impatiently rush to questions which a further study would have rendered unnecessary; and it is safe to say that the majority of "objections" raised to Theosophical teachings are such as could have been solved by the objector himself, had he been a genuine student. In the ordinary courses of education, scholars are required and are content, to accept provisionally many of the teacher's statements, in full confidence that further study will explain what in the beginning cannot be made clear. In the same spirit an earnest student of Theosophy will be wise enough to hold many of his difficulties in reserve, until, by further investigation, he has gained better acquaintance with his subject. In the case of those who are not willing to adopt these wise and patient methods of study, it may be reasonably questioned whether they are the more anxious to learn or to disprove.

Above all it is sought to make these Man-

uals such that they shall appeal to the heart
and not *merely* to the head; that they shall
be of practical service to the reader in the
problems of his daily life, and not mere intellectual exercises. For there have been in
past days books written by persons more distinguished for a certain grade of mental nim-
bleness than for heartfelt devotion to the cause
of truth; and these have appealed only to
those people who love intricate philosophical
problems better than practical work. But,
as H. P. Blavatsky so frequently urged, the
message of Theosophy is for suffering humanity; and the great Teachers, whose sole purpose is to bring to mankind the Light of
Truth and the saving grace of real Brotherliness can have no interest in catering for
the mental curiosity of merely a few well-
to-do individuals. Even soulless men, said
H. P. Blavatsky, can be brilliantly intellectual; but for those who are in earnest in their
desire to reach the higher life intellectual
fireworks alone will have little attraction. We
intend, therefore, to keep the practical aspect
of the teachings always to the front, and to
show, as far as possible, that they are what

they claim to be — the gospel of a new hope and salvation for humanity.

These Booklets are not all the product of a single pen, but are written by different Students at the International Headquarters of the UNIVERSAL BROTHERHOOD AND THEO-SOPHICAL SOCIETY at Point Loma, California. Each writer has contributed his own quota to the series.

For further explanations on Theosophy generally, the reader is referred to the Book List published elsewhere in this volume and to the other Manuals of this series, which treat of Theosophy and the various Theosophical teachings.

CONTENTS

I

THE UNITY OF TRUTH

THEOSOPHY is another name for the ancient "Wisdom-Religion." But Theosophy is not *a religion* in the ordinary meaning of that word; it is rather the ancient Wisdom which comprised science, philosophy, and religion. This Wisdom may be considered, as to its source, under two aspects. It is the voice of the Divine in man; or it is the teaching of men who have progressed so far on the path of progress that they have become divine, *i. e.,* the mind has become one with the higher consciousness of the God within. Consequently, all Great Souls, or Great Teachers, are men who have reached that high plane which the Bible calls "the unity of the Spirit"; and their teachings must agree in essence, though the forms they assume may vary from age to age. It also follows that the teachings of such advanced Beings, and the divine voice in each of us, must harmonize, for the Divine is One, is Wisdom itself, and all its teachings must be in harmony. No argument is needed to convince any one who understands Theosophy in this light, that it must be the " mother of religions." But all do not understand Theosophy in this light. Some look upon it as a mere cult invented by H. P. Blavatsky; though she herself repeatedly asserted, as did Jesus, " my teaching is not mine, but his that sent me." (John vii. 16). Others have regarded Theosophy as only a recrudescence of old heresies. These objections to Theosophy are mutually destructive; for it is a logical law that contradictories may both be false, but cannot both be true.

For all those who harbor such misconceptions it is necessary to place before them some evidences that will appeal to the reason; though true conviction springs rather from the inner higher nature of man than from the mere mental perception of things. Hence the old saying: He who is convinced against his will is of the same opinion still.

The teaching given out by H. P. Blavatsky did not originate with her. Not only does she assert this very plainly, declaring that she presents "a nosegay of culled flowers, and only the string is hers that ties them" (*The Secret Doctrine*, I, xlvi); but the whole trend of her writings is to remove the veils from the various teachings given in past ages, East and West, and to show the true harmony, the essential unity, both in nature and in purpose, underlying all those teachings, when rightly understood.

It would not, however, be just to H. P. Blavatsky, nor to the message given through her, to suppose it to be merely a repetition of some ancient teachings to be found in various philosophies or religions. It should be clearly understood that she has made a great advance upon the past. The world today needed that the ancient Wisdom-Religion should be given out more fully than on former occasions, and this H. P. Blavatsky has done.

Of course she has given out but a small portion of the "*Gupta Vidyâ*," the "Secret Doctrine," yet what she has given out is more than the world, at present, is advanced enough to assimilate in its fulness. The tendency of the modern mind along scientific lines, with a strongly materialistic bent, necessitates that this aspect of the Ancient Wisdom should be brought forth to meet the needs of the age. Consequently many things about the nature and origin of man and of the world, not to be found elsewhere, are given out in *Isis Unveiled*, in *The Secret Doctrine*, and in H. P. Blavatsky's other writings.

In the time of Jesus there was little need for modern scientific teachings, and they were not given *as a system of technical knowledge*. Then moral and spiritual teachings, and a life which was an embodiment of these, was the thing especially needed. This line of teaching is still needed, and will be for a long time to come, but something more is required now. The advances made in geology, astronomy, and other branches of science, called for more light on those lines, and this has been given. The teachings given out by H. P. Blavatsky are really a *revelation,* in the old sense of the word; they are the unfolding of what the ordinary mind could not of itself have discovered. Yet, the truths, the facts, always existed for those whose divine nature was able to see them, and to impress this knowledge on the recipient intellectual nature.

It will thus be seen that the claims of Theosophy are very large; larger indeed than the horizon of our present knowledge; for it distinctly affirms that the revelations which have been given are only a portion of that vast treasury of knowledge which we shall yet explore; and which, even now, is known to our Elder Brothers, who are the real Custodians of the Divine Wisdom-Religion. In other words, all existing religions have presented only a fragment of the TRUTH. Some religions, or systems of philosophy, have emphasized one aspect of Truth, others another aspect of it, according to the state of the world at the time. As man is a Soul, the great need of ordinary mankind in every age has been moral and spiritual; therefore all religions have, in varying degrees, ministered to the moral and spiritual progress of mankind. But in addition to this, some have contained a strong philosophical element, others a more practical element. It was not, however, until our own day that what is called the scientific element has been made publicly prominent, as it has been in *The Secret Doctrine* and in other writings by H. P. Blavatsky. While, according to her own statement, she has given out to the world but a small portion of that vast wisdom of which her Teachers are the Custodians, yet she has given enough to stimulate the mind of scientific men all over the world for the remainder of this century, and longer.

It is well known to students of Theosophy that already not a few things which H. P. Blavatsky revealed in her writings have been confirmed by the investigations of the learned. And no doubt many of the things not as yet accepted by scientific men will be corroborated in the not distant future. Already every new find in the domain of archaeology and in kindred branches of science, is tending to vindicate H. P. Blavatsky's teaching regarding the great antiquity of humanity. The very dwarfed notion of chronology which prevailed in the West, owing to mistaken views of the Bible, is passing away. A saner conception of evolution is gaining ground as the result of the great light·which Theosophy throws upon man's past. A sounder knowledge of psychology is possible as a result of what we now know of man's sevenfold nature, and of the various lines of his evolution. In a very true sense we have revealed unto us new heavens and a new earth. Before the close of this century the world will awaken to the wonderful revelation which has been given in the Theosophic unfoldment of the present age. Then there will be no need to prove that Theosophy is the mother of religions, for the fact will be recognized by all who are able to form a just judgment.

The great mission of Theosophy is to *unify*.

Universal Brotherhood is the unification of Humanity, and the Elder Brothers have planted its seed in the soil of the last century, and of this century.

Right knowledge, right feeling, right action: by these three chiefly will men be brought to realize that "Unbrotherliness is the insanity of the age," as Katherine Tingley has said. It is always most necessary to *live* Theosophy in order to lift humanity to something higher. And, as part of that right action, right feeling — a really kind and loving disposition to those we would help — must inspire it as its heart and life. But, *in addition to these all-important factors in genuine Theosophy, there is needed that extended knowledge which gives life a basis in sound philosophy.*

The more man advances the more he seeks to solve the riddle of existence. Corresponding to the notions of past, present and future, man yearns to know his own nature, whence he has sprung, and what is his goal. He also seeks some rational explanation of this universe of which he feels himself a part. To these questions Theosophy has in all ages given an answer, but today that answer is fuller than ever before. The Ancient Wisdom has always existed, and always exerted an influence upon the races of mankind through all the ages. While it is impossible to give in detail the workings of the great Theosophical Movement throughout the centuries, there are some things which are well known, and which cannot fail to bring conviction to the open-minded inquirer.

II

SOME OF THE TEACHINGS

AT the outset it may be well to state briefly some of the Theosophical teachings concerning the origin, nature, and destiny of man, and of the universe. This will give definiteness to the task of comparing the different religions and philosophies with each other, and will make it easier to connect them with their common source, the Ancient Wisdom-Religion.

One of the first and most important things which Theosophy places before us, is the *Law of Periodicity* which pervades the universe as a whole, and is seen in all its parts. The second thought is the *Unity of Being*. The going forth or manifesting of the One Life is called the Great Breath; and the out-breathing and in-breathing of man is a *type* of the outflow and return of the Divine Creative

Energy. Of course human language and human conceptions must be inadequate to deal with the Eternal, the Absolute; and this truth must always be kept in mind as we use the terms of the finite and concrete to speak of the Infinite. The One Absolute Life, or Being, is conceived as the source of what is called the Unmanifested Logos, or Word; which, in turn, produces the Manifested Logos, and returns unto Itself. From this Manifested Word, existence proceeds by definite stages, or planes, until we have, at last, this universe of suns and planets. This is the going forth of the Great Breath, or manifestation, or existence, or creation. The return of the Great Breath is the universal re-becoming one with the Absolute. Thus, evolution implies involution. Day and night, activity and rest, birth in the objective, and return to the subjective, these are the ways of Nature.

From this it follows that the Divine is immanent everywhere, and in all things; not as contained in them, but as the One Reality within, or behind, every appearance. With

startling force the words of the New Testament come before one's mind — " Because
I live, ye shall live also." (John xiv. 19).
Or the words of the *Bhagavad Gîtâ* — " I
established this whole universe with a single
portion of myself, and remain separate."
(Chap. x). It also follows that the Infinite
Plan, Wisdom, or Purpose, must be manifested on all planes of the universe. Or, in other
words, the great and the small, the macrocosm
and the microcosm must be images of each
other. "As above, so below," said the old
philosophers. " God made man in his own
image," says the Old Testament.

Theosophy has given a much fuller teaching
than was known to the world before, concerning the septenary nature of the universe, and
of all things therein. This truth was known
publicly to some extent in ancient times, as
we see from the number seven being so sacred
among the Hebrews, and also in India, Egypt,
and other countries. This is one of the special
ways in which the Divine Plan of the Universe
is stamped upon each of its component parts.

As the image of the sun is seen in each of the myriads of bubbles on the surface of the river, so is the Divine reflected in all. The Divine transcendence, and the Divine immanence, these are the two great and complementary conceptions of Life which sages have taught in all ages. In the present day the forward movement of thought seems to emphasize chiefly the fact of the Divine immanence; but in other ages the Divine transcendence was often dwelt upon almost exclusively. It is at this point that Theosophy renders such important service to the various great religions and systems of philosophy, by unfolding the fundamental truths which all contain in part, but which none manifest very clearly. It also gives us a rational conception of the universe, which avoids the dualism of some ancient philosophies, and reconciles the Divine transcendence, and the Divine immanence. In the *Bhagavad Gîtâ*, a Theosophical treatise, this immanence of the Divine is stated plainly; and yet there is no confining or limiting of the Infinite by the manifested:

I established this whole universe with a single portion of myself, *and remain separate.*

And again:

But there is another spirit designated as the Supreme Spirit — Paramâtmâ — which permeates and sustains the three worlds. As I am above the divisible, and also superior to the indivisible, therefore, both in the world and in the *Vedas* am I known as the Supreme Spirit.—(Chap. xv).

In the New Testament we have teaching that is very similar, and which has the ring in it of the ancient Wisdom:

For in him we live and move and have our being; as certain also of your own poets [*e. g.*, Aratus, and Cleanthes] have said, for we are also his off-spring.—(Acts xvii. 28)

For of him, and through him, and unto him, are all things.—(Rom. xi. 36)

The words of Paul in I Cor. xv, remind one strongly of that " Great Day Be With Us," which the Wisdom-Religion speaks of as the return of all to Absolute Being. Paul says:

Then cometh the end, when he shall deliver up the kingdom to God, even the Father. . . . Then shall the Son also himself be subjected to him that did subject all things unto him, that God may be all in all.

This is surely the return of the Great Breath, the end of one period of manifestation.

Theosophy, as revealed to us, deals with only a few points of the great Involution and Evolution. For instance, it deals chiefly with our solar system; and, more particularly with life on this planet during a portion of the Fourth Round; though many other things are touched upon in a general way so as to give mankind a rational conception of the Universe, and especially of human life on this planet. But the portion of the Wisdom-Religion thus revealed to us far transcends in fulness and in scope any and all existing teachings, and clearly points to the Ancient Wisdom as the great mother of religions.

In the course of ages the various religions wandered far from their source, and forgot, or almost forgot, that source. But we have now begun a movement toward UNITY on all lines. Comparative language, comparative literature, comparative religion; these and other similar studies indicate that the trend of thought is toward a recognition of unity as underlying all superficial differences of individuals, or of nations. Universal Solidarity is thus a movement towards that Great Center from which all have proceeded, and to which all must return.

In this return, or re-becoming, the definitely religious impulse or consciousness manifests itself in various ways. Religion may be likened to the homing instinct in some pigeons, which enables them, though in distant and strange places, to turn their flight homeward. Among men of various lands and ages we find expressions of this homing instinct. "Thou hast been our dwelling-place in all generations," says the Psalmist. And in Wordsworth we have a similar idea: "trailing clouds of glory do we come from God, who is our *home*." In the Gîtâ it is written, "Thou who art the dwelling-place of the universe"; and, "Thou art the final supreme receptacle."

ASPIRATION ONE WITH RELIGION

ALL real religion is at bottom this consciousness of the Divine, and the resistless aspiration of the Soul towards the Eternal. It is that celestial attraction by which our souls are moved and swayed in their courses, as the planets are in their orbits by the Sun. Religion is the great binding force. But we are conscious of another force in us, the impeding force of our lower nature. Therefore the message of all religions must be, how to cultivate or develop the true nature, the homing instinct in us, and how to overcome the hindering influence of the lower self.

The kingdom of heaven is within. Man is a temple of God. The purpose of religion is the unfolding of the heaven within, until it fills the world. Or, it is the manifesting of the Divine in man until the whole man is taken up into, or becomes one with the Divine. A true and clear perception of the purpose of life is most essential towards realizing that purpose. It is also of great importance to *know ourselves,* to *know what we are,* and *how* we have come to be what we are; to know the various principles of our constitution, that we may work intelligently towards the perfecting of our being. This scope is fully covered by the Wisdom-Religion, or Theosophy. It explains to us our origin, and the origin of the Universe. It explains, not only our duality, but our sevenfold nature; and shows us how man is a little image of the Universe and embodies in himself all the planes of the Universe, from Âtmâ, or pure Spirit, to the visible outer sheath, the material body. We are thus, at one and the same time, made aware of the Divine immanence, and of the Divine transcendence; and we are, therefore, the better able to explain and sympathize with the various aspirations and movements of the human mind as shown in the different forms of religion, from age to age, in different lands.

While we discriminate between those religions which keep closest to the great meaning and purpose of life, we are able to judge charitably even of those lower forms of religion which savor more of man's lower nature than of his higher. We call to mind the words of Krishna in the *Bhagavad Gîtâ:*

In whatever form a devotee desires with faith to worship, it is I alone who inspire him with constancy therein.

A similar expression is found in the book of the Acts:

Of a truth I perceive that God is no respecter of persons; but in every nation he that feareth him, and worketh righteousness, is acceptable to him.

What an amount of misery might have been averted if these words of Peter had always been kept in mind by professed Christians, and especially by that Church which leans so much on Peter!

Theosophy having thus made plain for us the nature and purpose of true religion, helps us the better to understand how it is that religions decline as they cease to minister to the higher nature of man, and become subservient to the lower self, or to selfishness, in some of its manifold aspects. For it is a lamentable fact, and one of the most prominent things in history, that religions in most, if not in all cases, very soon become deflected from the lofty spirit and purpose of their founders. This fact is well illustrated by the parable of the enemy who came and sowed tares among the good seed, while men slept. It is partly on account of this corruption which soon takes place in religions, that the ancient Wisdom-Religion needs to be again and again declared to the world in forms suited to human needs. The new revelation is new in its form, and in some of its details, but it is the Old Truth which has been from the beginning. H. P. Blavatsky clearly states that her message is not a new thing, but part of the Ancient Wisdom. We find in the New Testament a similar statement. St. John says he does not write a new commandment, but an old commandment which had been from the beginning, *viz.,* brotherly love. And in the East it is an ancient teaching:

Hatred does not cease at any time by hatred; hatred ceases by love; this is an *old* rule.

Religion, being in its essence the consciousness of the Divine, and the impulse or attraction towards Divinity, has ever largely con-
sisted, in its manifestation, of some means by
which this impulse might be realized. The
different "cults" are mostly modes or methods
by which men seek to realize the. purpose of
existence. However dimly recognized in some
cases, the object is one and the same, namely,
return to the Divine. H. P. Blavatsky says:

> There is not a religion, whether Christian or
> heathen, that is not firmly built upon the rock
> of ages — God and immortal spirit. (*Isis Unveiled*,
> I, 467)

Theosophy helps us to understand that all
religions have the same great goal in view.
This, of itself, should tend to remove the
prejudices that spring up in the various religions, and should help to foster a spirit of
unity among all who are striving towards the
same goal, whether they call it heaven, paradise, or by any other name.

THE ORIGINS OF RELIGIONS

THEOSOPHY also throws much light upon the origin of the various "cults"; for, by unfolding the original teaching, or some of it, we are helped very much in tracing many of the divergencies which have arisen.

It will be readily seen that among all religions the idea of *Sacrifice* has been very prominent. It is well known that the ordinary evolutionist looks to savage life as illustrating the genesis of modern man, and his cults. The savage personifies the forces of nature, and offers sacrifices to gain their favor. But Theosophy teaches that races, like individuals, have their periods of youth, maturity, and old age. The savage, in some cases at least, is but the decayed remnant of what was once a great race. It is said that the aborigines of

Australia are a remnant of the Third Root
Race, which, at its zenith, was much more
spiritual than the sub-races of the Fourth Root
Race. The idea of sacrifice has undergone a
long degradation, and it is only within the
last few thousand years that we find a gradual
movement away from gross notions of sacrifice to more spiritual conceptions. Even during the short space of Hebrew history, outlined
for us in the Old Testament, we see what a
hard battle the spiritual teachers had to wage
against the bulk of the people, and the materialistic tendency of the priesthood. And, in
this respect, Semitic history is a close parallel
to the history of India, Egypt, and every other
country.

In the Greek and Latin classics, from the
time of Homer onward, we find various kinds
of sacrifices mentioned. From the ancient
histories or relics of many countries we find
evidence that sacrifice of some kind was almost
universal. In some special cases human sacrifices were offered, but generally animals were
offered in sacrifice as a substitute. From very

early times the common articles of food were used as offerings. In later times the prophets declared that such offerings were not required; that the real and true sacrifice was the giving up of the lower nature to the higher. This was a return to something like the original meaning of sacrifice. Whatever hinders the return God-ward must be given up. The lower must give way to the higher; the animal nature to the god within. This is what is taught in the *Bhagavad Gîtâ:*

Some devotees give sacrifice to the Gods, while others, lighting the subtler fire of the Supreme Spirit, offer up themselves. (Chap. IV)

We have a similar teaching in Rom. xii. 1:

Present your bodies a living sacrifice, holy, acceptable to God, which is your reasonable (or spiritual) service.

The reasoning in this passage and in I Cor. iii, and elsewhere, is that we are temples of God, and therefore the whole of the tabernacle or temple should be sacred and holy, and devoted to the Divine Light of the Holy of Holies. The whole of life should be held sacred:

Whether therefore ye eat or drink, or whatsoever ye do, do all to the glory of God.

So also, in the *Bhagavad Gîtâ,* we are taught:

Whatever thou doest, O son of Kunti, whatever thou eatest, whatever thou sacrificest, whatever thou givest, whatever mortification thou performest, commit each unto me. (Chap. ix)

The spiritual meaning of sacrifice was always the inner teaching. The tendency to materialize figurative teaching is seen in regard to nothing more clearly than in this matter of sacrifice. In some of our modern Theosophical writings the language is highly figurative, as it was in the ancient teaching, and we can well imagine that a materialistic mind might very soon degrade the spiritual to the carnal. For instance, in *Light on the Path:*

Before the soul can stand in the presence of the Masters its feet must be washed in the blood of the heart.

In the light of this we may read that saying

in Heb. ix. 22, "Without shedding of blood
there is no remission." And we can see how
the religions of the world have perverted the
ancient teaching, and carnalized the great spiritual truth, that in the return God-ward, the
lower nature must be given up or consecrated
to the Divine Self within. St. Paul, being
acquainted with the ancient Wisdom-Religion,
spoke of "dying daily"; and being "dead unto
sin, but alive unto righteousness"; and felt
that "though the outer man perish the inward
man is renewed day by day." These and many
similar passages must be familiar to all; and
yet, lamentable and almost incredible though
it may be, it is nevertheless the fact that orthodox *Churchianity*, the world over, Romanist
and Protestant, is based on myths misunderstood, and symbolic language materialized.
The whole "scheme of salvation," in a few
words, is this: Adam, and all his descendants,
through him as their federal head and representative, became subject to death on account
of the broken law. Christ, the second Adam,
died in the room of humanity, and having paid

the legal penalty of physical blood, all who believe in him are saved, and all who do not are lost. Also, theologians have always maintained that the animal sacrifices of the Old Testament prefigured the (literal) perfect sacrifice of Jesus.

Slowly, very slowly, mankind is awakening from the nightmare of ages, the perversion of teachings which were once lofty and spiritual, into dogmas revolting to reason; but which in the name of religion ministered to the lower selfish element of man's nature, and were therefore popular or "orthodox" in all ages.

Nothing has been more degraded than the ideas of sacrifice, substitution, atonement, and yet, as is so often the case, great spiritual truths do exist of which the ordinary dogmas are hideous caricatures. Theosophy teaches today, as it did long before the dawn of ordinary history that the very universe exists through sacrifice, but *not* sacrifice which is a pain, or a penalty, as we commonly conceive it to be. It is taught that the great Helpers of Humanity sacrifice themselves for weaker lives. There is a passage in the first volume of *The Secret Doctrine* which is full of grandeur; it is where the SILENT WATCHER is spoken of as the GREAT SACRIFICE (p. 207).

It is he who holds spiritual sway over the *initiated* Adepts throughout the whole world. He is, as said, the "Nameless One" who has so many names, and yet whose names and whose very nature are unknown. He is *the* "Initiator," called the "GREAT SACRIFICE." For, sitting at the threshold of LIGHT, he looks into it from within the circle of Darkness, which he will not cross; nor will he quit his post till the last day of this life-cycle. Why does the solitary Watcher remain at his self-chosen post? Why does he sit by the fountain of primeval Wisdom, of which he drinks no longer, as he has naught to learn which he does not know — aye, neither on this Earth, nor in its heaven? Because the lonely sore-footed pilgrims on their way back to their *home* are never sure to the last moment of not losing their way in this limitless desert of illusion and matter called Earth-Life. Because he would fain show the way to that region of freedom and light, from which he is a voluntary exile himself, to every prisoner who has succeeded in liberating himself from the bonds of flesh and illusion. Because, in short, he has sacrificed himself for the sake of mankind, though but a few Elect may profit by the GREAT SACRIFICE.

It is under the direct, silent guidance of this MAHÂ — (great) — GURU that all the other less divine Teachers and instructors of mankind became, from the first awakening of human consciousness, the guides of early Humanity. It is through these " Sons of God " that infant humanity got its first notions of all the arts and sciences, as well as of spiritual knowledge; and it is they who have laid the first foundation-stone of those ancient civilizations that puzzle so sorely our modern generation of students and scholars.

And what is true on the higher planes is also true regarding the higher nature in each of us. The descent into human forms of the Sons of Light, about 18 million years ago, in the latter half of the Third Root Race, was the manifesting of the Higher Ego, or Christos, in man. For it is truly said: " We are temples of God and the spirit of God dwells in us." Man's nature being sevenfold, his evolution has been on several planes, and not on the physical alone, as the ordinary Darwinian supposes. The Christos in each of us has made the great sacrifice in descending into matter in order to guide, purify, and finally make one with itself the lower nature. This is the real at-one-ment, or atonement, of which the orthodox dogma is truly an awful misconception. The Christ is crucified in each of us, and must continue to be so until the lower nature is raised up, and made fit for union with the God within us. That is the great day of at-one-ment. Then we shall be able to say in our whole nature: " Not my will but thine be done." Then the sacrifice of the lower self will be complete; it will have ascended in the flame of perfect love. Then the soul can " stand in the presence of the Masters."

The universe is a continual " becoming." The descent of spirit into matter is the " fall of man." Man is himself the fallen angel. Jesus said, quoting from Psalm lxxxii, 6, " Ye are Gods, and all of you are children of the Most High," and he added, " the scripture cannot be broken." (John x. 35)

The ancient Wisdom-Religion may be found all through the Bible; and in the sacred writings of every great religion. The cross itself is one of the oldest symbols in the world. All history is a symbol. The life of each individual is a type of the whole. It must be so, as man is the little image of the universe; his sevenfold nature corresponding to the seven planes of the Cosmos. It need not then be wondered at that the story of Jesus the Christ is a picture of what takes place in the universe, and in each individual, nor need we marvel to find all Great Souls manifesting many points of likeness. St. Paul cried out, " I protest I die daily." There is a double sacrifice taking place in each of us; that of the Christos, which, like Prometheus, suffers, and is chained to matter as a result of bringing from heaven the celestial fire to hasten the evolution of the lower nature in man; and there is also the sacrifice of the lower self as it dies to its desires and passions and rises into the higher life of the spirit. The consciousness of the necessity of this sacrifice of the lower nature has led men in many lands to practise great austerities. Men, like Simon Stylites, have perched themselves on lofty pillars, or in some other manner have tried to separate themselves from their lower natures by separating themselves from the world. They have tortured the body thinking to develop the soul. This is a sad misconception of the truth. *The Voice of the Silence* says:

> Think not that breaking bone, that rending flesh and muscle, unites thee to thy " Silent Self." Think not that when the sins of thy gross form are conquered, O victim of thy Shadows, thy duty is accomplished by nature and by man. The blessed ones have scorned to do so.

Another phase of the same misconception is seen in those philosophical systems which regard matter as something evil in itself. It is " matter out of place," or anything out of place, which is the evil. The evil is when the lower nature seeks to drag down the higher nature, instead of being purified and lifted up by it.

IV

UNITY THE KEYNOTE OF THE NEW ERA

IT is often said that Theosophy does not oppose any religion as such, but seeks to enable each person to find in his own religion the primal truths which are one and the same in all religions. This is very true, and the subject of sacrifice illustrates this. Theosophy alone is able to explain the fundamental truths in this idea of sacrifice; and in so doing it helps us to see how misconceptions have arisen. There is the sacrifice of the universe, in which every step downward of the Divine Spirit into manifestation is a sacrifice. Or, to put it in another way, Spirit clothes itself in denser and denser sheaths. This is the going forth of the Great Breath. Redemption is the re-becoming, or the return Home. Each stage of the return is a sacrifice, the transformation of the lower nature into the higher, it is being born again not only by water, but also by fire. The lead is transmuted into gold. Each step upward, though a seeming death, is really not destruction, but transformation of life. Nothing is lost, or " cast as rubbish to the void."

Looking at the matter in this light, how sad the spectacle of men in many lands and ages offering up human sacrifices, or even offering up animals! Well might the prophet exclaim:

To what purpose is the multitude of your sacrifices? . . . I delight not in the blood of bullocks or of lambs. . . . Who hath required this at your hand to trample my courts? Wash you, make you clean. . . . Cease to do evil, learn to do well.— Isaiah i. 12, 17.

And again:

Is not this the fast that I have chosen? to loose the bonds of wickedness, to undo the bands of the yoke and to let the oppressed go free, and that ye break every yoke. Is it not to deal thy bread to the hungry, etc?—Isaiah lviii. 6, 7.

With a departure from the true original

meaning of sacrifice, there arose a false notion of that great law of the universe by which the higher sacrifices itself for the lower, in order to raise it to a higher plane. The selfishness of the lower mind, working on this for ages, elaborated a scheme of salvation in which, instead of the lower dying for the higher, *something else* should be *substituted* as a sacrifice. Finally, in modern orthodoxy, we have the sublimest facts of the universe degraded into mere legal transactions, in which the pure is by a fiction regarded sinful, and the sinner esteemed just. And yet Jesus himself taught the law of Karma plainly, and declared that the transgressor would go into a prison from which he could not emerge until he had paid " the very last mite."

Theosophy, the mother of religions, thus shows us the great fundamental truths, and enables us to see, in some degree, how the various religions have made turbid the waters of the perennial fountain of truth. Selfishness and misconception lie at the root of the false dogmas. In this day many have come to feel that these dogmas are not true, but it is by the help of the Wisdom-Religion that men are able to see the original fundamental truths and understand how, in so many cases, these truths have been forsaken and perverted.

The New Era in which we are fortunate enough to live, has as its key note or grand design, UNITY. The many tribes, races, families of mankind have gone to different parts of the earth, and each has developed certain qualities peculiar to itself. The time has now come for them to recognize that all are members of *one family;* and to join together in mutual enrichment, in harmonious unity; each, in this way becoming heir to the thousands of years of racial development achieved by the whole human family. Many things are working together to this end. On material lines the nations are being bound together by electric wires, and lines of communication, and unity of interests. Even so on inner planes, subtle currents are linking men together. The great things we did together in the long forgotten past will be eclipsed by the still more glorious achievements we shall unitedly accomplish in the Golden Age ahead of us. But among the things that tend to harmony and unification, nothing is more potent than *true* religion. And as we see that the ancestral Wisdom which we had about man and the universe is ours once again, we shall join hands, and the veil of covering shall be removed from all flesh, for we shall see eye to eye, and new pages of the Wisdom-Religion will unfold as we need them and are able to use them wisely.

To compare the ethics and ideals of the various religions with each other and with the Wisdom-Religion, is difficult, because most people have more or less prejudice in favor of some one religion; or if unprejudiced, each man naturally understands his own religion better than he can understand any other. Yet, notwithstanding these drawbacks, it is surely possible to make a fairly accurate survey of some of the great religions, or religious ideas, or symbols, for purposes of comparison.

On the question of ethics simply, it is not

difficult to point out the fundamental agreement existing between several of the great religions.   The moral law is much the same in
the commandments of Moses, and of Gautama
Buddha.   Truth, honesty, justice, purity, reverence for life, respect for parents, and the like;
these are the common principles of morality
in Christianity, Judaism, Hindûism, Buddhism,
Mohammedanism, and Confucianism.   Moreover, all great Teachers have recognized that
love is the foundation of law, and is the ful-
filment of the law.   Do unto others as you
would have them do unto you, is the positive
aspect of the great law as taught by Christianity.   Do not unto others what you would
not have them do unto you, is the negative
aspect of the same law of mutual consideration.   And the philosophic basis of the commandment is the *unity of life,* the unity of
humanity.   It is because we are many members
in one body, members one of another, and if
one member suffer the other members must
also suffer; it is because of this great fact
that it is wrong to injure anyone.   It is be-

cause of the unity of life that it is wrong to do anything to injure this unity — wrong to lie, or to steal, or to bear false witness. We call that thing wrong which is against the well-being or harmony of the whole, or any part of it.

The Jews recognized all sin as being first of all, against the Supreme Source of truth and right. Even in our· law courts we have still some echo of this idea existing. It is the " People," or the " King," as the case may be, against the person who is charged with an offense. With some nations the Supreme Source of all receded more and more into the background of human consciousness, and the void was filled in the popular fancy by a host of gods and goddesses which personified some of the powers of nature, or some of the faculties of the human soul. Idolatry, in its more and more material aspects, marks the *lowest point of the arc, not the primeval point from which we have started; that primeval starting point was the Wisdom-Religion.* This, of course, is entirely opposed to the ordinary views of modern science. But modern science, and modern history, begin where man begins to emerge from the lowest point of the cycle. Even the modern scientist believes that the finer and rarer precedes the denser. Our material earth is the last step in the process of materialization. The fluid, gaseous and ethereal states mark anterior stages of manifestation. If the scientists will only study the analogy of Nature faithfully they will be led to the portal of true Wisdom.

In maintaining the position that Theosophy is the mother of religions, it is necessary to distinguish between essentials and those things which are only external. Many things connected with the various cults have nothing Theosophic about them. They are modern; they are mere human accretions, or even perversions of the original teaching. Again, there are certain cults which may be regarded as having naturally sprung from the human mind viewing with awe and reverence the forces of nature. Yet even these, in their pure and primitive forms, were probably given by Great

Teachers, who used symbols to a large extent in their teaching; for, as H. P. Blavatsky explains,* those Great Teachers knew that words would be forgotten in the course of ages, therefore they used the picture teaching of symbols, which would be more easily preserved. Consequently the various cults, such as sun-worship, star worship, serpent worship, sex worship, tree worship, and nature worship generally, were at first pure and lofty. The symbolic was regarded as merely symbolic. It was only during the course of long ages that the symbolic teaching became gradually degraded as the human race itself sank deeper and deeper into materialism.

---

* *The Secret Doctrine,* volume I, page 473.

V

SEPTENARY NATURE AND MAN

AT all times the essential thing, lying behind all outward signs, has been a love of Perfect Truth, of Absolute Good; and a realization that man is truly the offspring of the Most High. Also, that the Divine Life is a Unity though seen in manifestation under a countless variety of forms. In a word, we should endeavor to realize the Divine as both transcendent, or above all, and immanent, or in all manifestation. This has always been the aim of the Wisdom-Religion, as manifesting through the Divine Principle in man; or through the express teaching of those Great Souls, who call themselves our Brothers, though they have developed far beyond ordinary humanity. It is this which gives the Wisdom-Religion its unique position and its strong claim upon us; it is the teaching of the Great Helpers of humanity, and it is also capable of verification as the real Self in each of us rises to the high plane of development which our Elder Brothers reached ages ago. But even beyond that, it is in a large degree capable of being demonstrated to the reasoning mind — a principle in us which is lower than the spiritual or divine Ego. For instance, when Theosophy tells us that man is sevenfold, and that nature is sevenfold, we have a teaching which our reason leads us to accept because we meet so many evidences of it. Nor does it require much demonstration to show that this teaching must have been given by ancient Sages, for we find it in the oldest religions. If we begin with the present and go backward, we shall be astonished at the amount of evidence existing.

We think of the seven days of the week, one of which is the day of rest, and we are at once reminded that in both color and sound the septenary law rules. There are seven notes in the musical scale, and seven prismatic colors. Human life is divided into periods of seven years. It is an old saying that man has seven senses, though only five are in use generally. Some philosophers have spoken of man as having seven obvious parts; and seven internal organs; and seven foci through which the soul acts. The seventh day, or the fourteenth, was regarded as critical for certain diseases. The human offspring is viable in the seventh month, and in the seventh year the child undergoes an important change, which some religions recognize, having borrowed it from the Ancient Wisdom. Life on the earth is powerfully influenced by the revolution of the moon in 4 times 7 days. Human life, as we see from Shakespeare, was divided into seven ages. These seven stages were closely associated with the seven planets of astrology. These are but a few of the instances in which we find the number seven very prominent in Nature.

Now, if we glance at some of the ancient religions, or races, we shall see how important a place was held by the number seven. From our Northern forefathers we have the seven

days of the week, and their names. Among
the ancients a symbol for the universe was
a ship with seven pilots. In India, says
Mr. Subba Ráo, it was taught that there
were six primary forces of Nature resumed in
a seventh. Among the ancient Greeks, Apollo,
the Sun God, was called the sevenfold or
ἑβδομαγέτης. Among the Persians the number
seven was held sacred to Mithras, the Sun
God. Plato tells us that from the number
seven was generated the soul of the world.
Among the ancient Hebrews the sacred ladder
had seven steps of ascent, the love of God;
and seven steps of descent, the love of one's
neighbor. On the ancient Assyrian tablets
were represented seven gods of the sky, and
seven gods of the earth. Among the Free-
masons seven members make a perfect lodge,
though five may hold one. Among the ancient
Aryans the number seven was sacred. There
were seven sages, seven planes of the universe, seven holy islands. In the Bible we find
seven as the sacred number, from Genesis
with its seven days, to the Revelation with

its seven churches, seven angels, seven candle-
sticks, seven trumpets, seven kings, seven vials
poured out. The seventh day, the seventh
month, the seventh year, and seven times seven,
the Jubilee, all show how Jewish national life
was permeated with the sacredness of the
number seven. The teaching that the *land*
should have its sabbaths, or rests, and not
only men and animals, indicates a profound
knowledge of nature, obtained either by direct
teaching, or as the result of long experience.
Modern science recognizes that the life of
metals, or machinery is prolonged by periodic
rests. And the lack of rest for the land is
diminishing very much the productiveness of
not a few parts of America, and of other
countries. The Hebrews, with good reason,
connected national well-being with keeping the
sabbaths. In so doing they were working in
harmony with nature, which, as Theosophy
shows, is sevenfold.

Now, if we examine this fact, that nations
so far apart should have the sacredness of the
number seven as a basic principle in life, and

in religion, we have a strong indication that they must, in some distant past, have obtained this knowledge from one and the same primal source — the ancient Wisdom-Religion. Let us turn to the exposition of the ancient wisdom, as given by H. P. Blavatsky in *The Secret Doctrine,* a work which she has written as a commentary on the ancient book of Dzyan. If this book of Dzyan, with the other ancient records, could be placed before the world, and if the mysterious ideographic characters could be read and could be understood by scholars, then nothing further would be needed to prove that the *Gupta Vidyâ,* the ancient hidden wisdom, was indeed the fountain of knowledge, the mother of religions. But this cannot be done. The ancient records are preserved with great care, and some of them are " accessible only to the *highest initiates.*" We must be thankful to H. P. Blavatsky for the sample she has given us, and still more so for her explanation of the translation. A few samples will show this.

In regard to the Universe, *before* the Great

Breath went forth, we read: " The Eternal Parent, wrapped in her ever invisible robes, had slumbered once again for seven eternities." " The seven sublime Lords and the Seven Truths had ceased to be." Then, at the beginning of manifestation we read: " The last vibration of the seventh eternity thrills through infinitude." " Then the three fall into the four. The radiant essence becomes seven inside, seven outside." From stage to stage of manifestation we find the sacred number seven. " Listen, ye Sons of the Earth, to your instructors — the Sons of the Fire. Learn, there is neither first nor last, for all is one: number issued from no number." " Learn what we who descend from the Primordial Seven, we who are born from the Primordial Flame have learned from our fathers." And again: " Thus were formed the Rûpa and the Arûpa: from the one light seven lights; and from each of the seven, seven times seven lights." All through the account of the genesis of the universe, or of this planet, the number seven is found. No wonder then that fragments, dim memories of the ancient teaching should be found in the Old Testament, in the sacred writings of India, Persia, Egypt, and of every other nation.

And when we turn to Anthropogenesis, the origin of humanity, we find the number seven very prominent. The earth is sevenfold, man is sevenfold. The earth passes through seven stages or rounds — we are now in the fourth. In each round there are seven Root Races, and in each Race seven sub-races. No wonder then that H. P. Blavatsky says,

Number Seven, the fundamental figure among all other figures in every national religious system, from Cosmogony down to man, must have its *raison d'être*. It is found among the ancient Americans, as prominently as among the archaic Âryans and Egyptians. — (*The Secret Doctrine*, II, 34)

The septenary nature of man, as taught by Theosophy, is thus seen to be in harmony with the basic number of the manifested universe. This was known to the ancient Egyptians, but it disappeared from ordinary teachings, at least in the West, during the time of a descending cycle. Modern languages have no terms for the seven principles of man; not until we go back to ancient Egypt and ancient India do we find names for these principles. In the New Testament, only a threefold division of man — body, soul and spirit — is given. And as a result of this we find St. Paul, and other writers, when speaking of the higher Manas and the lower Manas, much hampered to make their meaning clear. In the Old Testament we do not find a full account of all the human principles either; though in the esoteric teachings of the Hebrews, as appears from the Kabalah, they evidently had obtained, or preserved, part of the ancient Wisdom-Religion, as did the Egyptians and the Hindûs. This will be seen at a glance by comparing the two plates given in *Isis Unveiled* (ii, 264), where the ancient Indian and ancient Hebrew conceptions of the Universe very closely correspond. It may not be amiss to notice that between the obvious teaching of the Old Testament and the Hebrew esoteric lore, a vast difference exists.

VI

ESOTERIC AND EXOTERIC
TEACHINGS

IT is well known that there is very little, some have thought nothing, about the future life in the early part of the Bible. It is concerned about this life chiefly, and about right living here, not about the state of the soul after death. Keep the Commandments, that thy days may be long in the land, is the burden of the teaching. And if a modern Orientalist is correct in supposing that the Hebrews had an exoteric form of religion for the mass of the people, and an esoteric teaching for the "elect," it is only what we find to be the fact with other old religions also. This inner teaching was handed down orally to those selected to receive it. The "schools of the prophets" probably existed not only in the days of Elisha and of Samuel, but all

through the history of the Hebrew people.
It must have been always a difficult matter to
know when, and how much of this occult
teaching to give out to the world, or to the
mass of the people generally. While, on the
one hand it is wrong to withhold the bread
of life, or the light; on the other hand, as we
know from experience, it is a mistake to give
knowledge, or to try to give it, to men before
they are ready for it, before they hunger and
thirst for truth. And in all ages, so far as we
know, the Light-bringer was regarded as an
angel of darkness rather than an angel of
light. The writer of *The Secret Doctrine,* the
Harbinger of the Wisdom-Religion in our
own day, shared the same fate. " Which of
the prophets did not your fathers persecute? "

THE MYSTERIES

" THE MYSTERIES " is the term applied to
the secret wisdom which was handed down
from teacher to pupil under solemn promise
not to divulge it except in the manner in which

he himself had received it. In addition to this, it is evident that it was a matter of attaining to inward illumination, or spiritual development, rather than the mere imparting and receiving of knowledge. No doubt, according to the great law of Nature, as each higher plane helps that below it, the pupil was helped, and taught, and trained by his elders, but the end of it all was that he might attain to that condition in which he should know for himself. To know the truth really *he himself had to become one with it.* To tread the Path, he had to become that Path himself. To know God he had to become one with the divine within himself. This "Knowledge," from the very nature of the case, must have ever been, and must ever continue to be the " Great Secret." As knowledge is power, and as power may be used selfishly, it is easy to see why many things were kept hidden from the mass of the people. This was not to keep men in darkness, but to keep powerful instruments out of the hands of the selfish. Knowledge is a two-edged sword, and he who uses

it or any faculty unwisely, injures himself
even more than he injures others. Notwithstanding all the care used, much knowledge
was employed selfishly during the evil days of
the Fourth Race, the Atlantean, and the world
has not yet gotten rid of the bad effects.

These " Mysteries " were the outcome, or
the consolidation of the ancient Wisdom-
Religion which had long previously come to
man in the Third Race, the Lemurian, when
the Sons of Mind, the Mânasaputra, descended
upon earth and took upon them the human
form, becoming our spiritual ancestors. For
man being sevenfold, has a spiritual heredity
as well as a physical and an astral. From
many sources we get hints about the " Mysteries." Aristotle considered that the welfare
of Greece was secured by the Eleusinian Mysteries. Socrates says, " Those who are acquainted with the mysteries insure to themselves very pleasing hopes against the hour of
death, as well as for the whole of their lives."
Cicero writes, " When these mysteries are explained we prove not to have learned so much

of the nature of the Gods, as of the things themselves, or of the truths we stand in need of." Sallust tells us, " the intention of all mystic ceremonies is to conjoin us with the world of the Gods." Plutarch affirms that in the mysteries, " The First Cause of all things is communicated." One of the Christian fathers, Clemens Alexandrinus, writes, " The doctrines delivered in the greater mysteries are concerning the Universe. Here all instruction ends. *Things are seen as they are;* and Nature, and the things of Nature, are given to be comprehended." Plato says, " The design of the mysteries is to lead us back to the perfection from which, as a principle, we first made our descent." Again, he declared it was " difficult to find the Father and Molder of the Universe; and when found, impossible to discover him to all the world." We may compare this with what is written in the *Book of Job,* which is said to be a book of *initiation.* Job, when the climax of the whole drama is reached, declares, " I had heard of thee by the hearing of the ear; but now mine eye seeth thee." And in the book of *Ecclesiasticus* it is written, "At first, she (Wisdom) will walk with him by crooked ways, and bring fear and dread upon him, and torment him with her discipline until she may trust his soul, and try him by her laws. Then will she return the straight way unto him, and comfort him, and *show him her secrets.*"

Philo says of the Jewish teachers, "They changed the words and precepts of wisdom into allegories, *after the custom of their ancestors.*" Maimonides writes, "Whoever shall find out the true meaning of the book of Genesis ought to take care not to divulge it." In the ancient Egyptian Ritual we read, "This book is the greatest of all mysteries. Do not let the eye of anyone see it; that is detestable. Learn it. Hide it." In *Isis Unveiled* H. P. Blavatsky records much about the mysteries. We learn that whether in ancient Egypt, Greece, Persia or India, the object of the mysteries was much the same. "The unity of God, the immortality of the Spirit, belief in salvation only through our works, merit and demerit; are the principal articles of faith in the Wisdom-Religion, and the groundwork of Vedaism, Buddhism, Parseeism, and such we find to have been even that of the ancient Osirism, when we, after abandoning the popular Sun-God of the materialism of the rabble, confine our attention to the *Books of Hermes*, the thrice-great." In the books of Manu we find similar teaching: " The man who recognizes the Supreme Soul, in his own Soul, as well as in all creatures, and who is equally just to all (whether men or animals) obtains the happiest of all fates, that to be finally absorbed in the bosom of Brahmâ." " Of all the duties the principle one is to acquire the knowledge of the Supreme Soul (the spirit) ; it is the first of all sciences, *for it alone confers on man immortality.*" This reminds us of the words of Jesus (John xvii. 3), where he says that " to know the Father as the true God is eternal life." In the Persian *Desatir* it is written, " Whatever is *on earth is the semblance and* SHADOW *of something that is in the sphere;* while that resplendent thing (the prototype of the Soul-Spirit) remains in *unchangeable* condition it is well also with its shadow. But when the *resplendent one* removeth far from its shadow, life removeth from the latter to a distance. And yet that very light is the shadow of something still more resplendent than itself." (*Isis Unveiled*, II, p. 113) Proclus said, " in all the initiations and mysteries the gods exhibit many forms of themselves, and appear in a *variety of shapes*, and sometimes, indeed, a formless light of themselves is held forth to the view; sometimes this light is according *to a human form*, and sometimes it proceeds into a different shape."

From these " mysteries " the great religions of the world had their origin. As the mysteries were only for the few who had been tried and found worthy, a popular form of teaching, based upon them, was given to the public. This was, of course, symbolic; and the tendency of the lower mind in man is to drag down, and materialize things spiritual; hence the degradation of the mysteries, and the lapse into idolatry. For the essence of idolatry is ever the same, it is the worship of a sign or symbol instead of the thing represented by the symbol. Hence the great need from age to age, for Messengers, Teachers, Reformers to come and lift up the world to that light from which it has fallen. And this is true, though, according to the great law of Progress, the cycles of the world's life are on the whole onward and upward. We find this thought of restoration, or purification, prominent in several religions. In regard to Judaism, which directly or indirectly, has such a widespread influence on all Western nations, we find a notable hint given by Jesus on one occasion. Speaking of a certain custom, Jesus said that Moses permitted this because of the hardness of their hearts, but " *from the beginning it was not so.*" And as to the true Law, he said he came not to destroy the Law, but to fulfil it, or to fill it full of a deeper significance than they supposed it to possess. Again he said, they had "made the Law of none effect by their traditions."

VII

A CYCLICAL REGENERATION

IF we look at Brâhmanism and Buddhism, we shall find that S'âkyamuni came to *restore*, not to destroy anything really good and true. The primal teaching had, through long ages, been made of none effect by a declining sacerdotalism; just as the teaching of the Mosaic Law had been through Phariseeism. There was need for renewal, rebirth, restoration. Hence, one of the Great Teachers, one who had much to do with giving the Wisdom-Religion to this generation, said that *"pre-Vedic Budhism"* was the teaching which he and his companions proclaimed. This can only mean the ancient Wisdom-Religion, the heritage given by the Sons of Light, when the lands and seas of the world were very different from what they now are.

As Brâhmanism declined, S'âkyamuni came

to enlighten and restore; and met the natural opposition of a declining priesthood. But in the course of time Buddhism also declined, and a restoration was needed. This was only partially accomplished by various great teachers; so that a real return to the *"pre-Vedic* Budhism" is needed for modern Buddhism as well as for Brâhmanism. This fresh re-issue of the waters of Truth from the ancient source is afforded in Theosophy.

Among the Israelites Moses came to teach and purify, but in the course of ages the Scribes and Pharisees "sat in Moses' seat"; and made the law of none effect. Jesus came to restore, to lead men back to the light; but before long the various ecclesiastical divisions obscured, and well-nigh buried out of sight the teaching of Jesus. Therefore, according to the Great Law that guides the progress of the world, a new Teacher had to come in the Nineteenth century. She came to a world needing the life-giving light of the Spirit, instead of materialism. She came to give new impulse and right direction to a world that was

wandering far from the true Path. She came
to give, on a vaster scale than had ever been
given before, a new revelation embracing
Cosmogenesis and Anthropogenesis, Religion,
Science, Philosophy — the revelation of the
universe to man, and of man to himself; this
was the scope of her mission. And her revelation, as she herself says, was not her own,
but was simply a portion of the great Wisdom-
Religion, while more remains to be given out
at the end of the Twentieth century, or at
some future time, as man becomes ready for it.

It is according to wisdom that in a declining cycle certain truths are not given out.
The septenary nature of man and of the universe is one of these simple yet basic truths,
and it was not given out during the Dark
Ages. We have now entered on a new age,
an ascending cycle, and that makes possible
the increase of light. Yet, even so, knowledge
is being used selfishly, and consequently to the
hurt of humanity; but working in harmony
with the Life and Purpose of the universe
we may with open vision, like the prophet of

old, see that "they that are with us are more than they that are with them." We may realize the truth of the words of the New Testament, "Greater is he that is in you than he that is in the world."

THE VALUE OF EACH RELIGION

THE various religions which have sprung from their parent, the Wisdom-Religion, though they have failed in many respects, in every case have accomplished something. Just as races, or nations, or individuals, have separate messages to give, so each religion has its separate note to sound in the complete harmony of the whole.

The well-known author, James Freeman Clarke, in his *Ten Great Religions,* has made an attempt to indicate what the various religions failed in doing, and what they severally accomplished. "The essential value of Brâhmanism," he says, "is its faith in spirit as distinct from matter, eternity as distinct from time, the infinite as opposed to the finite, sub-

stance as opposed to form." But, he thinks,
it does not explain the world, it simply denies
it.   He thinks it is incapable of morality, of
true worship, and also that it does not really
teach immortality because it neglects the absolute distinction between right and wrong,
and teaches absorption instead of immortality.
The system of Confucius he regards as having
done good work in teaching morality; in its
reverence for the past; and in its respect for
useful institutions.   Buddhism, he says, "has
done good in teaching the relation of the soul
to the laws of nature; its doctrine of conse-
quences (Karma), and its promise of an ultimate salvation in consequence of good works."
But he regards it as having "the defect that
belongs to all legalism."   The religious teachings of the Eddas, and of Zoroaster he groups
together because "they both recognize the evil
in the world as real, and teach the duty of
fighting against it.   They avoid the pantheistic
indifference of Brâhmanism, and the absence
of enthusiasm in the systems of Confucius and
Buddha."

The Semitic religions, Judaism, Christianity, and Mohammedanism, proclaimed a pure monotheism, and consequently it was only after contact with Persia that we find in the Jewish scriptures any mention of an *evil principle,* and then it is not the Satan of orthodoxy, but rather the heavenly critic who appears among the sons of God, as stated in the book of Job. A *perfect* conception of the Divine transcendence precludes the notion of a Devil. In Egypt, as in northern Europe, the divine was seen chiefly in the various powers of nature. In Greece the divine was seen in man rather than in nature.

The form of religion known as "ancestor worship," was, and to some extent still is, very wide-spread. It was also very ancient. Not only China and Japan, but Greece, Rome, and nearly every part of the world has seen this form of religion. It was no doubt one of the early shoots from the Wisdom-Religion. It seems to have sprung from several elements, one of which was the knowledge that in his real nature, man is an immortal spirit. Another element was, that between the Absolute and our present humanity, countless orders of finite beings exist. It was also a perpetuation and an extension beyond death of parental relationship and was, therefore, rooted in natural affection. The wonderful persistence of it is seen in the East; and it is said that the public devotion to the "ancestors" recently shown by the Emperor of Japan has done much to strengthen the ancient religion, which neither Buddhism nor any other teaching has been able to stamp out.

VIII

TEACHING BY MYTHS AND SYMBOLS

THE study of myths and symbols has been very suggestive of an earlier and more universal religion than any now existing. The wide-spread influence of certain myths, and the fact that certain symbols have been found in lands far apart and belonging to times very remote, point to a common origin in a prehistoric past. Of these symbols the cross, in its various forms, is of great antiquity. In *The Secret Doctrine,* Vol. II, p. 557, we read:

Verily may the Cross be traced back into the very depths of the unfathomable Archaic Ages. Its Mystery deepens rather than clears, as we find it on the statues of Easter Island — in old Egypt, in Central Asia, engraved on rocks as Tau and Svastika, in pre-Christian Scandinavia, everywhere!

In *The Secret Doctrine,* Vol. II. page 99,

H. P. Blavatsky says that the Svastika form
of cross has many meanings:

In the *Macrocosmic* work, the "HAMMER OF CREA-
TION," with its four arms bent at right angles, refers
to the continual *motion* and revolution of the invisible Kosmos of Forces. In that of the manifested
Kosmos and our Earth, it points to the rotation in
the cycles of Time of the world's axes and their
equatorial belts; the two lines forming the *Svastika*
✠ meaning Spirit and Matter, the four hooks
suggesting the motion in the revolving cycles.
Applied to the *Microcosm,* Man, it shows him to be
a link between heaven and Earth, the right hand
being raised at the end of a horizontal arm, the left
pointing to the Earth. . . . It is not too much to say
that the compound symbolism of this universal and
most suggestive of signs contains the key to the
seven great mysteries of Kosmos.

In ancient Scandinavia it was the hammer of
Thor. Dr. Schliemann found it in two forms
under the ruins of ancient Troy.

The symbol of the *Tree* was also very ancient, and universal. Among the Scandinav-
ians it was *Yggdrasil*, the tree of Existence.
Among the ancient Hindûs it was Aśvattha,
the world-tree. In Egypt the sycamore tree

was sacred to Hathor. In the Bible, from the first of Genesis to the last of Revelation, we find the tree frequently used in a symbolical sense. The tree of the knowledge of good and evil, and the tree of life are in the Garden of Eden. And in the heaven of the Apoca-. lypse, the tree of life bears fruit every month, and its leaves are for the healing of the nations. In the ancient writings of the Wisdom-Religion the Sons of MAHAT are quickeners of the human Plant. (*The Secret Doctrine*, II, 103)

The *Sun*, as we might naturally expect, was in all lands, and from the most ancient times, regarded with great reverence. In a simple untutored race it would be quite natural to expect men to show reverence to the source of light and life. One of the first white men to come into contact with the natives of the distant interior of South Africa tells how they bowed to the sun as he rose above the horizon, " because he warmed them." But between this simple and very natural form of gratitude, and the elaborate conceptions of Egypt and of other ancient lands, a vast difference exists.

Mr. Owen Morgan, as quoted in *Egyptian Belief and Modern Thought,* says:

It is a common error to suppose that the ancients worshipped the sun. They did nothing of the kind. They worshipped the Eternal Spirit, which in Egypt went under the name of Osiris, and in Britain under the name of Celi, the *concealed;* and regarded the sun as the first-begotten of the Father, and of the inert confusion of matter.

Mr. Bonwick quotes from the Vedas, the Upanishads, and the Yasna Avesta of the Persians, severally, as follows:

Let us adore the supremacy of the Divine Sun, the Deity who illuminates all, from whom all proceed, are renovated, and to whom all must return; whom we invoke to direct our intellects aright in our progress to his holy seat.

And from the Upanishad:

It is I, O Brahmâ, who adore thee under the form of the resplendent sun. O sun, eternal, hearken unto my prayer!

The Avesta calls the sun "without beginning and without end." Kennedy, speaking of the Hindû religions, says that the sun "appears under two perfectly distinct characters; the

one as the Supreme Being, the other as the
inferior deity, the regent of the "solar orb."
In the course of ages the symbol became in
itself an object of worship. Thus idolatry
originates, and it assumes various forms. It
is the worship of the letter rather than of the
spirit. It is the tendency to materialize where
we should look to the spiritual, or ideal. It
is narrowing and limiting, where we should
ever study to reach upward to the limitless
and the supreme. Yet, as the human mind is
constituted, for the vast majority of mankind
at least, forms must be used to give definiteness. To the Magus, whom Sir E. Arnold, in
The Light of the World, makes say:

> Om, Amitâya! oh,
> The Immeasurable! What word but doeth
> wrong
> Clothing the Eternal in the forms of Now?
> Our great Lord Buddha would not name Him
> once,

Mary of Magdala replies:

> If no name be,
> Will not the weak soul say, "naught is to
> name."

But the tendency of worship through forms, has in most cases been, not to open up vaster and wider heavens to the adoring vision, but rather to place the worshipper with his back to the light, so to speak, and to make the objects of his worship, images, or shadows, of himself, more and more limited and material. This is as true of so-called Christians today as it was of the Chaldæans thousands of years ago. "God is spirit," said Jesus, "and to worship truly we must worship in spirit and in truth."

The fact that the prophets of Israel were loud in their denunciations of the idolatry into which solar symbolism had degenerated, did not prevent their using such expressions as "The Lord God is a sun and shield," (Ps. lxxxiv), "The sun of righteousness shall arise with healing in his wings." (Mal. iv) And in the New Testament we find in Rev. xix, these words, "And I saw an angel standing in the sun." Solar symbology is not only widespread, but exists to our own day in forms little suspected. For writers on symbology tell us that the pointed pyramid, or obelisk, is a solar symbol, and is seen in the spires and pinnacles of old churches; even as it is seen in Lapland, ancient Egypt, ancient America, ancient India, and China. Even the weather-cock has the same significance; the cock, according to Pausanius, being sacred to the sun, as the herald of the day. And in the symbolic writing of the Chinese this symbol is used. Du Halde, Vol. II, says " They, the Chinese, in representing the sun put a cock in a circle."

And as regards myths, if we have the patience to trace them to their source, they will lead us back to the origin of religions and races; back to that ancient time when there was one great religion, the Wisdom-Religion, which was the synthesis of science, religion, and philosophy — Divine Wisdom, truly, for it had its origin in the Divine Teachers, and in the Divine Self within Humanity.

The *mythos* was an ancient form of teaching. Like the story, or parable, or symbol, it expressed much — revealing truth to the wise and hiding it from the foolish — and it was a form of teaching easily remembered. The myths of Prajâpati, of Prometheus, of Osiris, all carry us back to the Wisdom-Religion, which alone can fully explain them. They all have the same message concerning the Divine in man. They all point to human progress and to the return of man and the universe to the Infinite Source whence all things proceeded.

The creation legends, the legends of fallen angels, and of giants, are all the broken lights that have come from the Wisdom-Religion. The story of Atlas takes us back to Atlantean times, and even to the Lemurian age, when the mountain range was thrice its present height, and when it might be said to support the heavens.

There is, however, one point which it is well to note carefully. H. P. Blavatsky tells us that in the Wisdom-Religion, the mythos or symbol had not one key only but *seven* keys. It is the tendency of some learned writers who are acquainted with but one key, the physiological, or the astronomical, to im-

agine that their explanation covers the whole
ground, and to ride their particular theory to
death; whereas a wider knowledge would give
a sounder view of Nature as septenary.

Through long ages of separation, each family, race, or religion, has treasured its own
form of the primal Wisdom, and has come to
regard all other forms as false. This is a
great mistake, but like most drawbacks, there
has been this compensating influence; it has
given intensity and devotion to the adherents
of each system. It is a fact well known to the
careful student of religions or sects today,
that not infrequently, the narrower the creed,
the more deeply in earnest are its adherents;
and often, too, the more illiberal a sect is intellectually, the readier are its adherents to
give and suffer for their narrow faith. While
on the other hand, a broad and liberal form
of thought is often accompanied with lack of
intensity and lack of liberality to give for it,
and suffer for it. When the river is narrow
it moves along with great force, and cuts a
deep channel; but when its waters broaden

out over many acres the stream loses in energy and can hardly turn a single mill. But the time has now come for mankind to find unity; to realize that all religions have had the same Mother — the Wisdom-Religion; to realize that all nations and all men are rays of the same Divine Being; and that by seeking this unity we shall progress to a higher plane of life. For Paradise regained is more than Eden restored. When we get to a point in the ascending cycle corresponding to the Third Root Race we shall have attained not only to great heights of spirituality, but also to that Wisdom which comes through many aeons of experience. In other words, the ascending angels on the great ladder reaching from earth to heaven, will be superior to those descending.

DOGMATIC TANGENTS

IN maintaining that Theosophy is the mother of religions, it is not claimed that *all* forms of religion have sprung from the ancient Wisdom. It is well known that the modern orthodox teaching in the West holds to the doctrine of Creation, that is, making out of *nothing*, in the strict sense of the term. It denies the dictum *ex nihilo nihil fit*. It declares that the *emanation* theory of the East is false. On this point, at least, an irreconcilable difference exists between modern western religions and the ancient Wisdom-Religion. And yet a proper understanding of the Eastern teaching about *Mâyâ* might serve to show how western orthodoxy arose. In the *Bhagavad Gîtâ* Krishna declares that:

Though myself unborn, of changeless essence, and the lord of all existence, yet, in presiding over nature — which is mine — I am born but through my own *Mâyâ*, the mystic power of self-ideation, the eternal thought in the eternal mind.

Some of the uses of the word *create* in the Old Testament may refer to this power of *Mâyâ*, or causing to appear; for example in Is. xlv: "I form the light, and *create darkness*. I make peace, and *create evil*." Darkness and evil are not positive entities, but only the shadows cast by Light, and by Good.

And it is worthy of note that the text which is specially quoted as proving *creation* to be distinct from making, only proves that the present order of things was not the source of things in the beginning — " By faith we understand that the worlds (aeons) have been framed by the word of God, so that what is seen hath not been made out of things which do appear." (Hebrews xi. 3) This passage, which speaks of aeons being framed by the Divine Word, is only another illustration of how the Wisdom-Religion underlies all religions. And when these religions understand themselves they will realize how much they owe to the Ancient Wisdom.

This is not the place to speak of Karma and Reincarnation, except to point out that these integral parts of the ancient teaching can be easily seen to be the workings of Nature. We see the law of seed-time and harvest, and whether we like it or not, " we reap the seed we sow, the hands that smite us are our own." What we call *Law* is a mode by which the One Life acts. And as to Rebirth, it will be found that those who object to it do so because they do *not view life from the standpoint of the soul, but from that of the body.* As the body has many days and nights, so has the soul in the long journey, and when the goal of all manifestation is reached, and the GREAT BREATH returns to ITSELF, the result of all the billions of years of progress is not annihilation. We do merge, or become one with the Eternal Parent, but we go forth again as the Divine Word of a new period of manifestation, after the " Seven Eternities."

As men realize the unity of their origin, and the unity of religion underlying all existing differences, it must tend powerfully towards real and lasting harmony and peace. We are many members in one body. We are all rays from the GREAT SUN. In our heart of hearts we can feel that the great primal truths of justice, uprightness, compassion are our common heritage, because they pertain to the ONE SPIRIT which is over all, and through all, and in us all.

There is no Religion Higher than Truth

The
Universal Brotherhood
and
Theosophical Society

Established for the benefit of the people of the earth & all creatures

OBJECTS

This BROTHERHOOD is part of a great and universal movement which has been active in all ages.

This Organization declares that Brotherhood is a fact. Its principal purpose is to teach Brotherhood, demonstrate that it is a fact in nature and make it a living power in the life of humanity.

Its subsidiary purpose is to study ancient and modern religions, science, philosophy and art; to investigate the laws of nature and the divine powers in man.

* * *

THE UNIVERSAL BROTHERHOOD AND THEOSOPHICAL SOCIETY, founded by H. P. Blavatsky at New York, 1875, continued after her death under the leadership of the co-founder, William Q. Judge, and now under the leadership of their successor, Katherine Tingley, has its Headquarters at the International Theosophical Center, Point Loma, California.

This Organization is not in any way connected with nor does it endorse any other societies using the name of Theosophy.

THEOSOPHICAL

MANUALS

XVI

FROM CRYPT TO PRONAOS

AN ESSAY ON
THE RISE AND FALL OF DOGMA

The Aryan Theosophical Press
Point Loma, California
1908

THEOSOPHICAL MANUALS

XVI

FROM CRYPT TO PRONAOS

AN ESSAY ON THE RISE AND FALL OF DOGMA

BY

(REV.) S. J. NEILL

The Aryan Theosophical Press
Point Loma, California
1908

COPYRIGHT, 1908, BY KATHERINE TINGLEY

PREFACE

THE remarks under this head are intended to be introductory to each of the Manuals.

First, as to the spirit in which they are offered. These Manuals are not written in a controversial spirit, nor as an addition to the stock of theories awaiting public approval. The writers have no time to waste in arguing with people who do not wish to be convinced, or who ridicule everything which is new to their limited outlook. Their message is for those who desire to know — those who are seeking for something that will solve their doubts and remove their difficulties. For such, all that is needed is a clear exposition of the Theosophical teachings; for they will judge of the truth of a teaching by its power to answer the questions they ask. People realize, much more now than in the early days of the Theosophical Society, the value of Theosophy;

for the ever-increasing difficulties engendered
by selfishness and materialism, by doubt and
the multiplicity of theories, have created an
urgent demand which it alone can satisfy.

Again, it is necessary to state clearly and
emphatically the genuine teachings of Theosophy, as given by the Founder of the Theosophical Society, H. P. Blavatsky, and her
successors, William Q. Judge and Katherine
Tingley. For, as H. P. Blavatsky predicted,
there are persons who have sought to pervert
these teachings and turn them into a source
of profit to themselves and their own selfish
and ambitious schemes. The true teachings
do not lend themselves to such purposes; their
ideals are of the purest and most unselfish.
Hence these persons have sought to promulgate under the name of Theosophy a perverted
form of the teachings, from which Brotherliness and other pure motives are omitted, and
which contains doctrines which H. P. Blavatsky showed to be maleficent and destructive.
As these pseudo-Theosophists have gained a
certain amount of notoriety by using the names
of the Theosophical Society and its Leaders,
it is necessary to warn the public against them

and their misrepresentations. Their teachings can easily be shown, by comparison, to be directly contrary to those of H. P. Blavatsky, whom they nevertheless profess to follow. Instead of having for their basis self-sacrifice, self-purification and the elevation of the human race, these teachings too often pander to ambition, vanity and curiosity. In many cases they are altogether ridiculous, and only calculated to make people laugh. Nevertheless, as these travesties have served to discredit the name of Theosophy and to keep earnest inquirers away from the truth, it is well that the public should know their nature and origin. They are the work of people who were at one time members of the Theosophical Society, but who did not find in it that food for their own personalities of which they were really in search. So they turned against their teachers in wounded pride and vanity, and started little societies of their own — with themselves at the head.

The writers of these Manuals have no personal grievance against any such calumniators. Inspired by a profound love of the sublime teachings of Theosophy, they have made it

their life-work to bring the benefits which they have thereby received within the reach of as many people as possible. And they feel that they will have the hearty sympathy and co-operation of the public in exposing folly and bringing the truth to light.

Theosophy strikes unfamiliar ground in modern civilization, because it does not come under any particular one of the familiar headings of Religion, Science, Philosophy, etc. into which our age has divided its speculative activities. It dates back to a period in the history of mankind when such distinctions did not exist, but there was one Gnosis or Knowledge embracing all. Religion and Science, as we have them today, are but imperfect growths springing from the remnants of that great ancient system, the Wisdom-Religion, which included all that we now know as religion and science, and much more. Hence Theosophy will not appeal to the same motives as religion and science. It will not offer any cheap and easy salvation or put a premium upon mental inactivity and spiritual selfishness. Neither can it accomodate itself to the rules laid down by various schools of modern thought as to

what constitutes proof and what does not. But it can and does appeal to the Reason. The truth of doctrines such as Theosophy maintains, can only be estimated by their ability to solve problems and by their harmony with other truths which we know to be true. But in addition to this we have the testimony of the ages, which has been too long neglected by modern scholarship, but which is now being revealed by archaeologists and scholars, as H. P. Blavatsky prophesied that it would in this century.

It may perhaps be as well also to remind those who would criticise, that the state of modern opinion is scarcely such as to warrant anybody in assuming the attitude of a judge. It would be quite proper for a Theosophist, instead of answering questions or attempting to give proofs, to demand that his questioners should first state their own case, and to be himself the questioner. The result would certainly show that Theosophy, to say the very least, stands on an equal footing with any other view, since there is no certain knowledge, no satisfying explanation, to be found anywhere.

Since the days when the wave of materialism swept over the world, obliterating the
traces of the ancient Wisdom-Religion and
replacing it by theological dogmatism our religions have had nothing to offer us in the way
of a philosophical explanation of the laws of
Being as revealed in Man and in Nature.
Instead we have only had bare statements
and dogmatic assertions. The higher nature
of man is represented by such vague words
as Spirit and Soul, which have little or no
meaning for the majority. The laws of the
universe are briefly summed up under the
term " God," and all further consideration of
them shut off. Then came a reaction against
the dogmatism of religion, and man pinned
his faith to knowledge gained by study and
reflection, limiting his researches however to
the outer world as presented by the senses,
and fearing to trench upon the ground which
dogmatic theology had rendered the field of
so much contention. The result of this has
been that neither in religions nor sciences,
have we any teaching about the higher nature of man or the deeper mysteries of the
universe. This is a field which is left entirely

unexplored, or is at best the subject of tentative and unguided conjectures.

Until, therefore, religious teachers have something definite, consistent, and satisfactory to offer, and until science can give us something better than mere confessions of nescience or impudent denials with regard to everything beyond its own domain, Theosophy can afford to assume the rôle of questioner rather than that of questioned, and does not *owe* anybody any explanations whatever. It is sufficient to state its tenets and let them vindicate themselves by their greater reasonableness; and any further explanation that may be offered is offered rather from goodwill than from any obligation.

Theosophy undertakes to explain that which other systems leave unexplained, and is, on its own special/ground, without a competitor. It can issue a challenge to theology, science, and other modern systems, to surpass it in giving a rational explanation of the facts of life.

Again, there are some questions which it is beyond the reach of the human mind, in *its present stage of development*, to answer; and it would scarcely be just to arraign Theosophy for not answering these.

Judgment should in all cases be preceded by careful study. There are always those who will impatiently rush to questions which a further study would have rendered unnecessary; and it is safe to say that the majority of "objections" raised to Theosophical teachings are such as could have been solved by the objector himself, had he been a genuine student. In the ordinary courses of education, scholars are required and are content, to accept provisionally many of the teacher's statements, in full confidence that further study will explain what in the beginning cannot be made clear. In the same spirit an earnest student of Theosophy will be wise enough to hold many of his difficulties in reserve, until, by further investigation, he has gained better acquaintance with his subject. In the case of those who are not willing to adopt these wise and patient methods of study, it may be reasonably questioned whether they are the more anxious to learn or to disprove.

Above all it is sought to make these Man-

uals such that they shall appeal to the heart
and not *merely* to the head; that they shall
be of practical service to the reader in the
problems of his daily life, and not mere intellectual exercises. For there have been in
past days books written by persons more distinguished for a certain grade of mental nim-
bleness than for heartfelt devotion to the
cause of truth; and these have appealed only
to those people who love intricate philosophical problems better than practical work. But
as H. P. Blavatsky so frequently urged, the
message of Theosophy is for suffering humanity; and the great Teachers, whose sole purpose is to bring to mankind the Light of
Truth and the saving grace of real Brotherliness can have no interest in catering for
the mental curiosity of merely a few' well-
to-do individuals. Even soulless men, said
H. P. Blavatsky, can be brilliantly intellectual;
but for those who' are in earnest in their desire to reach the higher life intellectual fireworks alone will have little attraction. We'
intend, therefore, to keep the practical aspect
of the teachings always to the front, and to
show, as far as possible, that they are what

they claim to be — the gospel of a new hope and salvation for humanity.

These Booklets are not all the product of a single pen, but are written by different Students at the International Headquarters of the UNIVERSAL BROTHERHOOD AND THEOSOPHICAL SOCIETY at Point Loma, California. Each writer has contributed his own quota to the series.

For further explanations on Theosophy generally, the reader is referred to the Book List published elsewhere in this volume and to the other Manuals of this series, which treat of Theosophy and the various Theosophical teachings.

CONTENTS

I

HUMAN VEILS OF TRUTH

RELIGION and dogma — are they both
necessary to us? Are they in the Grand
Design of things, as are spirit and matter, substance and form? And if so, what
should be their relation, or proportion to each
other? Some philosophers have thought that
" good " and " evil," " light " and " darkness,"
are necessary to each other, and these philosophers might equally well maintain that a
proper admixture of religion and dogma, with
a little ritual added, is as necessary for man's
well-being as are the various elements in the
air we breathe. Certainly the admixture extends throughout history, and it is probably
prehistoric. It is also common to all lands
and peoples, and might claim, with far more
justice than a certain church, to be accepted
"quod semper, quod ubique, quod ab omnibus"

— always, everywhere, and by all. But old age and universality do not make a thing right, else many vices might claim to occupy high positions, higher even than the dogmas.

Some words, and " dogma " is one of them, have a very innocent colorless youth, but in their old age they become sadly degenerate. It would have saved the world much sorrow and bloodshed if " dogma " had retained its original meaning of " opinion." But it did not do so. It became, says the *New English Dictionary:*

a belief, principle, tenet; especially a tenet or doctrine authoritatively laid down by a particular church, sect, or school of thought; sometimes, depreciatingly, an imperious or arrogant declaration of opinion.

From the same authority we learn that one of the earliest instances of the use of the word in English is in 1638, where we have the expression, " The grosse fanatick Dogmataes of the Alcoran."

To speak of the "rise and fall of dogma" covers a wide field. And it may seem rather strange to talk of the *fall* of dogma when there are still so many millions in all parts of the world whose religious systems contain so many dogmas; and when a certain church in the enlightened West is trying to " put back the clock " at the present moment by prohibiting the clergy and the laity from reading any books of a progressive character. Nevertheless, the Twentieth century will witness, as the Nineteenth century also in some degree witnessed, the declining power of dogma: for, as true religion becomes stronger the influence of dogmas must decrease and in the end disappear. By this it is not meant that the time is near when opinions or beliefs will cease. Men must always have opinions and see things somewhat differently until the light of *perfect* knowledge is reached. But, dogmatism, or the domination of certain dogmas over the minds and lives of men, will weaken and vanish. The freedom in which we now rejoice is possible because the dogmatic spirit has lost the power it once had to crush out freedom of thought; though in many quarters the attempt is still made to shackle the minds of men,

not only in the domain of religion, but in other
fields also.

The history of all religions presents very
much the same phenomena in regard to the
growth and influence of dogma. Very soon
after the good seed is sown the enemy comes
by night and scatters tares; and not infrequently the tares outgrow the wheat. But the
worst of it all is, that with many foolish people, the tares are mistaken for the wheat —
dogma is prized more than, or instead of, true
religion. Strange as this may seem, it nevertheless has had a clear illustration in regard to
the great Founder of Christianity himself. It
is well known that his teaching is not only devoid of dogmatism, but is of such a character
that dogma could not easily be built up upon it.
For, who could build a dogma on, " Blessed
are the peacemakers"; " Blessed are the pure
in heart"; " Be ye therefore perfect as your
Father who is in heaven is perfect"? Consequently, two sets of men have fallen into a
similar error in regard to the Sermon on the
Mount, and other teachings of Christ. The

unspiritual man says it is morality only, and that is the whole of religion; while certain orthodox teachers declare that the teaching of Christ is morality only, and not the real heart of religion, to get which, they say, we have to go to the epistles, and the full development of dogmas. And in harmony with this is the fact that a much larger number of sermons are based on the epistles than upon the words of Jesus himself. But is it not strange, as a pro-phet of the Nineteenth century remarked, that he who *himself came to be the gospel,* should have failed, in his longest and fullest dis-course, to preach the gospel and should have left this to be done by his disciples! This attitude, which for many centuries was the prevailing spirit of Christianity, shows how prone men are to prefer dogma to the true spirit of religion. Moreover, it helps us to see how dogma has grown up; and the origin of dogma or its relation to true religion, is indicated by the first words of the title to this essay — "From Crypt to Pronaos." This phrase is used to indicate a literal and historical fact; and it is also used figuratively to represent the process of thought as it proceeds from within outwards, and becomes more and more externalized and materialized.

Man, in his three-fold nature of spirit, soul, and body, is not only a type of the universe, but is also a symbol in which we see the process of unfoldment from within outwards. If the term *crypt* be regarded as the hidden center, the inmost of things, or the spirit of things, and *pronaos* the last, or outermost court of the temple, we shall have a picture of religious history in most cases. The dogmatic stage will correspond to the last, or outermost sheath of the soul, the outer court of the temple.

The history of these terms, *crypt,* and *pronaos,* is itself full of interest and instruction. In tracing historically the English use of the word crypt, the *Oxford English Dictionary* gives the earliest appearance of the word as being in 1432: " The cripte of Seynte Michael in the mounte Gargan." This use of the word is rare, the Latin form being the one commonly employed. Historically, the word is used (a) "as a grotto or cavern; (b) as an underground cell, chamber, or vault, especially one beneath the floor of a church used as a burial place, and sometimes as a chapel or oratory." In 1563 a writer says: "Christians had caves under the ground called cryptae, where they for fear of persecution assembled secretly together." In 1789 Brand writes: "The chancel of the church stood upon a large vault or crypt."

Of course the use of the word in its Latin form is much older. The term *crypta* was applied to a vaulted building partly, or wholly beneath the level of the ground. Juvenal speaks of the *crypta Saburae*. Seneca calls the tunnel north of Naples *crypta Neapolitana*. And Jerome uses the same term in speaking of the Catacombs.

According to the learned Venables in the *Encyclopaedia Britannica*, the crypt, as part of a church, had its origin in the subterranean chapel erected on the tomb of a martyr. When the tomb was not wholly below the

ground the part of the church floor over it
would be raised. This fashion of raising the
chancel or altar end of a church, to indicate
the crypt underneath, was widely imitated
even where the reason for it did not exist.
In nearly every country in Europe the remains
of ancient crypts exist, some of them being
of Roman workmanship.

H. P. Blavatsky, in the *Glossary,* tells us
that some crypts were for initiation, others for
burial purposes:

There were crypts under every temple of antiquity.
There was one on the Mount of Olives lined with
red stucco and built before the advent of the Jews.

And in *The Secret Doctrine* we read:

There were numerous catacombs in Egypt and
Chaldaea, some of them of a very vast extent. The
most renowned of them were the subterranean crypts
of Thebes and Memphis. The former, beginning on
the western side of the Nile, extended towards the
Libyan Desert, and were known as the *Serpent's*
catacombs, or passages. It was there that were performed the sacred mysteries of the *kuklos anagkes,*
the "Unavoidable Cycle," more generally known as
the "circle of necessity." (Vol. II, p. 379)

Again, the same writer says (*op. cit.*, 588, *note*) that there are "crypts in cis-Himâlayan regions where Initiates live, and where their ashes are placed for seven lunar years." From various sources we have statements to the effect that there are vast Crypts in the East in connexion with Gonpas. One of these is referred to in *The Secret Doctrine*:

In all the large and wealthy lamaseries there are subterranean crypts and *cave-libraries,* cut in the rock, wherever the *gonpa* and *lhakhang* are situated in the mountains. . . . Along the ridge of Altyntagh, whose soil no European foot has ever trodden so far, there exists a certain hamlet, lost in a deep gorge. It is a small cluster of houses, a hamlet rather than a monastery, with a poor-looking temple in it, and one old lama, a hermit, living near by to watch it. Pilgrims say that the subterranean galleries and halls under it contain a collection of books, the number of which, according to the accounts given, is too large to find room even in the British Museum. (*Introd.* p. xxiv.)

II

THE WISDOM-RELIGION

THAT the Wisdom-Religion existed during pre-historic ages, and that there are proofs of this in a " complete chain of documents," H. P. Blavatsky confidently affirms. It is only by the aid of such documents, hidden in " secret caves and crypts," that much of the ancient writings, such as the Vedas, can be made intelligible. The initiates do not keep these books from the world through any policy of selfishness, but because to give out some of the things which they contain to a race of men steeped in selfishness would be like " giving a child a lighted candle in a powder magazine."

The fact is not sufficiently kept in mind by some would-be teachers that after all, there is a power behind the visible course of events that makes real progress in all ages and lands depend on moral and spiritual growth.

In the course of modern progress we stumble onwards over the ruins of empires, frequently deaf to their voice of warning and instruction. It is possible to advance to a certain length in knowledge, or in power, but unless the moral and spiritual elements of our nature develop in harmony with the intellectual powers harm is sure to result; and in the end there will be a withdrawing of those powers which by their selfish exercise produced injury in the world. The earth is strewn with the wrecks of great nations, and great civilizations, because they were not built on the true foundation of the development and rule of the Higher Self in man. The Custodians of Wisdom have seen great material developments again and again crumble into dust. They have watched the new growths rise upon the dust and ashes of the past; and they know that the real progress of the race is always menaced by the giving of light before the eyes are ready for it; by the giving

of power before the divine man within has
sufficient control of the lower man to prevent
the power from being used selfishly. Knowledge leads to power, and knowledge used
selfishly injures humanity. Therefore it is
the duty of the Custodians of the Secret Wisdom to keep knowledge for those who are
ready or fit for it, and for them only. A
Theosophical book says:

Desire power ardently. Desire peace fervently.
Desire possessions above all. But those possessions
must belong to the pure soul only, and be possessed
therefore by all pure souls equally, and thus be the
especial property of the whole only when united.
Hunger for such possessions as can be held by the
pure soul, that you may accumulate wealth for that
united spirit of life which is your only true self.—
Light on the Path, p. 6

The fact that civilizations have grown up
and perished, and that others have slowly and
painfully risen upon their ruins has led many
learned authors to find the beginnings of religious life and worship in the rudest and sim-
plest forms existing among some semi-savage

races. The Secret Wisdom points us to many cycles of progress and decay before that age began which our wise men believe to be the first, and from which they trace existing forms of religion. The learned editor of the *Encyclopaedia Britannica*, Professor Robertson Smith, in his work on the *Religion of the Semites*, p. 180 says that

the great natural marks of a place of worship are the fountain, the tree, and grottos and caves in the earth. At the present day almost every sacred site in Palestine has its grotto, and that this is no new thing is plain from the numerous symbols of Astarte worship found on the walls of caves in Phoenicia. There can be little doubt that the oldest Phoenician temples were natural or artificial grottoes, and that the sacred as well as the profane monuments of Phoenicia, with their marked preference for monolithic forms, point to the rock-hewn cavern as the original type that dominated the architecture of the region. (cf. Renan, *Phénicie*, p. 822)

But if this be so, the use of grottoes as temples in later times does not prove that caverns as such had any primitive religious significance. Religious practice is always conservative, and rock-hewn temples would naturally be used after men had ceased to live like troglodytes in caves and holes of the earth.

Closely connected with this theory about caves or crypts is the fact that recent archae-ological investigation has shown a tendency to find a chthonic, or earth-origin for many dei-ties, even some which were supposed to be wholly celestial. Mr. Farnell, in vol. iv of his great work on the *Cults of the Greek States,* holds that Apollo was not at first a Sun-god, but a god connected with the earth, for in the early Greek cults there is little to connect him with the sun. Afterwards he became a War-god; and still later a Sun-god, resigning the war-lordship to Mars.

The cave or crypt may have been in some places early associated with a sacred shrine, especially if it happened to be a rent in the earth which sent forth hot air, or steam, or warm water, or peculiar vapors; but these facts carry us only a short distance into the past, and they do not explain the vast under-ground passages connected with ancient tem-ples in Egypt, India, and elsewhere, in which occult teachings were given. Robertson Smith regards the altar, the place of offerings, as the real origin of the sanctuary. Now this was in the outer court or *pronaos,* and may have been the symbol of exoteric religion; but it was not the true center or heart of the temple. Yet even this may have had an inner meaning; it may have spoken, to those whose ears were open, of the necessity for offering up the lower nature on the altar of sacrifice in the *pronaos* before the inner shrine could be approached. However, no doubt, to many it was the beginning and end of religion; just as to very many people today externals are the sum total of religion. It must be borne in mind that ancient temples were regarded as the homes of the Gods, and not as places of worship in the sense of modern churches. In most countries the temple was comparatively small, though there were some large ones, as the temple of Artemis at Ephesus, that of Hera at Samos, and some others. Dr. Seyffart says that

Only temples like that at Eleusis, in which the celebration of the Mysteries took place, were in-

tended to accomodate a large number of people.
The great sacrifices and banquets shared by all
the people were celebrated in the court of the
temple (περίβολος) which included the altars for
sacrifice, and was itself surrounded by a wall with
only one place of entrance.

From the description given of the Jewish
Tabernacle, and afterwards of the Temple,
no one can fail to perceive that a perfect system of symbolism existed throughout. The
outer court, the holy place, and the most holy
place, roughly corresponded to the three-fold
character of some Greek temples, viz. the *pronaos*, the *naos*, and the inner chamber (ὀπισθό-
δομος), which was behind the image, and
where valuables were kept. The *pronaos*, or
outer court, was the place of offerings.

There can be no doubt that the triple nature
of man as body, soul, and spirit was signified
by this form of Tabernacle and Temple. The
Holy of Holies corresponded to the *Âtmâ-
Buddhi* or Divine Spirit in man. Man was
regarded as the little image of the universe;
and the temple, with its three divisions, was

a type of man, " the temple of God." A story is recorded of a celebrated Rabbi who was mocked by a heathen for supposing that the Most High could be regarded as present in the Jewish Holy of Holies. The Rabbi brought forth a very large mirror and a very small one, and held them before his antagonist, asking him what he saw. The man answered that he saw a very large image of himself in the one mirror, and a small image in the other. Thus, said the Rabbi, do we regard the Universe and the Holy of Holies as both revealing the image of the Most High.

Nature herself continually reminds us that there is an inner aspect to all things. The molecule, the atom, the electron, or whatever name we may give the ultimate of matter on this plane, suggest an inner life, and an inner meaning everywhere. Why should the *pro-naos* of Nature's great temple contain for us the whole of what is worshipful? There is no fear that we shall exhaust the marvels and teachings she has in store for us. When we reach the holy place in any department of truth, and veil after veil is removed — as in the Tabernacle — there will remain veil after veil behind.

The movement of light and life is from the center outwards. The development of wisdom has been from the most holy place to the outer court. The teaching is in parables, that, as Swedenborg explains, men may see a certain measure of truth without the danger of profaning what as yet they are unable to appreciate fully. For, as Jesus taught, to cast pearls before swine is to be guilty of a double folly; they will trample them underfoot, and then they will turn and rend the giver.

Looking at history as Theosophy presents it to us, not as having emerged from barbarism about ten thousand years ago, but as a vast succession of waves, with hollows between, we may at first imagine that the work of the Great Teachers of the past has been one continual failure. How puny the wisdom of today compared with that of the Sons of Light in the Third Race! How far short do we come of the material progress of the Fourth Race in

its palmy days! How much has Egypt declined from the time of the early divine rulers!
How much has India gone backward! The
greatness of Chaldaea is marked by shapeless
ruins. Is this continual declination to mark
for ever the history of humanity? Why were
the Mighty Masters of Wisdom impotent to
bequeath a growing light to future ages; and
to prevent a corruption of the Mysteries? We
may answer this when we understand why the
shadows of evening lengthen, and why the sun
gives less warmth in winter, and why all things
have their spring-time and their winter.

The process of creation or manifestation, is
from the spiritual towards the material, and
then back again to the spiritual. This is the
character which is stamped upon all things.
Birth and youth, manhood and old age, are
not accidental things in Nature. And if the
decline of the Ancient Wisdom were to be continuous we might well be pessimistic. If the
process were to be always towards materiality the world would be a huge mistake. But
it is not so. The darkness breaks, here and

there it is shot through with shafts of light. When the lowest point of darkness or materiality is reached, then the Sun of Life and Progress begins to turn, and there will again be springtime and summer. We know this is the way of Nature in the smaller cycles of our common experience, and we may rest assured that the same great law extends throughout those realms of the manifested universe which as yet we can grasp by intuition rather than by scientific knowledge or intellectual sight.

III

THE SOURCE AND RISE OF DOGMA

NO form of teaching, it would seem, can be guarded absolutely against the risk of misconception. Words often change their meanings, and can easily be misunderstood in the course of time. Teaching by actions which are symbolical, or by pictorial representations, cannot secure to future ages a correct understanding of the meaning of those symbols, or of the suggestive actions. The Egyptian hieroglyphs in the *Book of the Dead* had already become extremely doubtful when later writers gave in the margin their explanation. And to the ordinary reader today the later explanation is often quite as enigmatical as the mystic characters which it attempts to elucidate. The same is true, though in a much smaller degree, in the case of the Hebrew Talmud; the ancient writing being in the middle of the page, and the explanation around it. And in the case of the Bible, or even of Greek and Latin classics, who does not know that where a real obscurity occurs in the text the commentators not infrequently leave it more obscure? As to symbolical acts, the things done by Jesus the Christ at the Last Supper are regarded in very different ways by Romanists and extreme Ritualists from what they are regarded by other professing Christians.

Now creeds and dogmas must be viewed in this light. They are, first of all, the presentation in the outer court, so to speak, of deep spiritual truths. Then the process of materialization becomes more or less rapid until we have a crystallization into church dogmas. It is a process similar to the Cosmic process from the fire-mist to earth or solid rocks. Thus the defect of all dogmatic systems is an incurable defect. Or, it can be cured only by the return to that from which the materializing process took its origin. But, besides this, there are other defects in the dogmatizing process which might be, in a great measure, prevented. The dogma-creating spirit is essentially the action of the lower *manas,* or lower mind. It is not simply that it is an attempt to give form and materiality to the Infinite, or the Spiritual, it is the mind, as apart from feeling, giving things its own embodiment.

Now, it is a strange but well-known fact, that no perfect agreement is possible between men so long as truths are viewed from the standpoint of the intellect only, whereas, all men instantly agree on matters of the heart. We can see the truth of this by supposing any good action done before men of the most dissimilar mental status. They will all at once recognize that it is a good thing to help those in distress, to save a person from drowning, or from being burnt. But no two people, very likely, have quite the same idea of God, or would explain any great spiritual truths in quite the same way. Therefore the mischief of creeds and of men being dominated by them, springs from a radical error. Unity, for ordinary men, can never be reached on the plane of the brain-mind. We agree as to what is good, but we cannot reach the same unanimity in regard to what is true, except, perhaps, in geometry or mathematics. And, still further, the creeds have nearly always changed natural ideas into ideas bounded by merely human-legal relations. Christianity has suffered in this way owing to the fact that a Latin spirit took the place of the Greek spirit. A well-known, and even orthodox professor in Great Britain has said that the change from the Greek *nomos* to the Latin *lex* aptly indicates the change that came over the spirit of early Christianity. Truths, from being vital or natural principles, as the Greek conception favored, became legal in the sense of a Roman law-court. This vast and radical change of spirit runs through all the centuries, and it may be called the spirit of petrifaction that has changed the living tree into a stone. No wonder then that the Professor just mentioned declares that Christ has been buried for over 1000 years in sacramentarian theories, dogmas, and even in the Bible itself.

No doubt Christianity has retained, though in a changed form, many Greek ideas, as it has borrowed many things from other sources; but the Latin spirit became the spirit of theology, of dogma, and creeds; and the mystic, spiritual element, like the dove sent forth by Noah, found no resting place. Nor did the Reformation cure this lamentable condition of things. The hard dogmatic spirit sprang up in Protestantism as much as ever it had done in the Roman church. And, while there were great and good men, men with spiritual aspirations in many places, their voices were drowned in the general clamor for dogmatic teaching. And even yet the dogmatic spirit rules in the churches, though there have been many hopeful signs during the last forty years or so of a return to the spirit of Jesus. But the creeds and dogmas will die hard, for they are entrenched in rich endowments, and fortified by trust-deeds and all the machinery of ecclesiastical courts. The dying process is sure to come, however; indeed, it is already here. The knell of dogma has sounded. Humanity is moving on the ascending cycle. The great Theosophical Movement, which has never ceased through the ages, is now moving like the birth of Spring, both in the East and in the West. A brighter day is near for those who sat in darkness and in the shadow of death. The time for the prisoners to become free, and for the fetters of creeds and dogmas to fall from the souls of men that they may walk forth in a large liberty and do the works of righteousness, has now come.

Although the birth and decline of dogma in the Western world claim our attention chiefly, it must not be supposed that human nature and the history of religions have been very different in the East from what they have been in the West.

In Europe, church missionaries, for reasons of policy, incorporated native ideas in the new teaching. The old cults baptized with new names made the work of conversion much easier and quicker. Jesuit missionaries in the East, in more recent times, carried this principle of accommodation to such a length that

even Rome thought they were going too far
— the line had to be drawn somewhere!

Similar phenomena may be observed in the
case of other religions. There is the growth
of eccclesiastic power. There is the with-
holding of knowledge from the people — for
knowledge leads to power — in order that the
people may be more pliant, and more easily
ruled by the hierarchy. There is also the
natural tendency of the lower human nature
to drag down things spiritual to the material
plane; and then, on the part of the teachers
there is an insensible, but constant giving way
to this worldly tendency in order that ecclesiastical control may be more easily maintained.
It has ever been the temptation to gain influence for religion by worldly means. This
was part of the temptation of Jesus — worship
me and your laudable object of saving humanity will be gained in the shortest and easiest
way, all the kingdoms of the earth shall be
thine. This temptation has existed in all ages,
and it is all the more powerful and dangerous,
because, in its first stages at least, it is related

to a true principle of conduct. When a re-
former or teacher wishes to uplift, or help any
portion of humanity, he must, of course, put
himself on the plane of those he wishes to
teach or help. He must be born. He must
come to them. He must not antagonize them.
He must accommodate himself, and his teaching also, to their needs and capabilities. All
this is very simple, and it is very easily seen,
and it is most reasonable. But it is just on this
matter of accommodation that the ground becomes slippery. As a matter of necessity
Truth is veiled to the finite comprehension.
The danger is in keeping the same veil too
long, instead of gradually withdrawing it in
order that a more spiritual perception of the
Truth may be reached by the people generally.
If this were done the process from the outer
court to the holy place would be natural and
continuous. But in most cases the symbol, or
representation, has been allowed to degenerate
or materialize the conceptions of the worship-
ers instead of becoming an avenue of more
light. This is, in a word, the history of the

growth of dogma. It is the growth of the
material, the outward, instead of the spiritual.
The history of religions is an illustration of
this. Even in modern history we see it clearly
presented. From the days of the Puritans,
say, until now, what a change there has been
in giving way to the pleasure-loving side of
men's natures. No doubt the Puritan was
wrong in supposing that joy was to be ban-
ished, and that sour looks and ways were vir-
tuous. But, consider now how the lower nature is petted and-pleased. In how many cases
do we not see the bribing of the lower nature
to get people to attend church and become
religious, or appear to be so! While it is not
the part of wisdom to antagonize those whom
we would uplift, it is not the part of wisdom
to pander to the lower natures of those whose
lower natures we wish to purify and transmute
into perfect oneness with the Higher Self
within.

This fundamental conception lies at the root
of all religions. It has to be seen clearly if
we would trace the working of Truth and

Justice in the education of humanity. Every revelation veils while it reveals. The danger is when this is forgotten, and when the imperfect and impartial representation is taken for what is perfect. We read that in the Jewish tabernacle the ends of the staves which were in the rings of the Ark protruded so that the veil which concealed the most holy place was pressed outward. This was a continual reminder to all who saw it, that the Ark *was there* behind the veil. In all religions the thought should be kept in mind that the symbol is only a symbol and not the thing itself; that the dogma or creed is only an imperfect, tentative presentation of deep spiritual truths as seen by imperfect minds; and that the creed or dogma is capable of revision, and should be revised from time to time. An old writer says, " Words are the wise man's counters, but they are the money of fools." The same may be said of all attempts to put in concrete form what is spiritual. To the wise man it is a symbol only, a reminder of the truth, but to the foolish it takes the place of reality. This limiting, materializing, or crystallizing tendency, this mistaking of the outer court for the holy place, is a great danger to which mankind has been liable through all the ages, and it is a danger still. The temptation to imagine that perfection has been reached, or that the complete Truth has been attained is one which we need continually to guard against. It has always ministered to the feeling of self-content, or self-sufficiency to think — " We have the only true religion, the only correct doctrine " — and men in all lands and ages have thus been hindered from further progress. Closely related to this is the tendency to condemn others. We need the wider outlook and the larger heart to enable us to regard all men as our brethren, and learners in the same great School of Life.

IV

DIFFERENT DOGMAS OF BAPTISM

IF we begin with the life of man in the flesh we shall see that from birth until death he has been encased in dogmas. Baptismal regeneration is first in order of time. With some churches baptism is said to make the child " an heir of God, and an inheritor of the kingdom of heaven." It was the strange fiction of the church that the child came into this world under the power of evil. Instead of thinking with Wordsworth that " heaven lies about us in our infancy "; or that " trailing clouds of glory do we come from God, who is our home," the Council of Trent confirmed the dogma of centuries, that " from the fall of man till his baptism, the Devil has full power over man, and possesses him by right." This gives the priesthood a very powerful control over the parents, and also over the child

from the very beginning of life. If the child
is born with an evil spirit which has to be cast
out, and the priest is the only person who can
exorcise the evil spirit, then it goes without
saying that the priest must be all-important,
and baptism of the utmost necessity. If the
dogma be true, no father or mother could wish
to neglect such a miraculous rite as this. There
is a double exorcism of the evil spirit, first
when the priest says, " come out of this child
thou evil spirit, and make room for the Holy
Ghost "; and afterwards at the font when the
priest again exorcises the evil spirit, and rubs
a little of his own spittle with the thumb of
his right hand on ear and nostril, saying, " be
thou opened " (*ephphatha*), in imitation of the
action of Jesus (Mark vii, 34). Then, after
anointing with oil in the form of a cross between the shoulders, and calling on the child
to renounce the Devil and all his works, the
priest pours holy water thrice on the child's
head in the name of the Trinity.

Did the church get this elaborate rite from
Jesus, or the early apostolic practice, or did

it concoct the thing partly out of its own fancy, and partly out of scraps of ancient religions? Anyone can see from the New Testament what a simple thing baptism was. We read that great crowds went out to the baptism of John, " Jerusalem, and all Judea, and all the region round about Jordan, and they were baptized of him in the river Jordan, confessing their sins." (Matt. iii, 5.) In the days of the apostles, " repent and be baptized, every one of you," are the words which St. Peter is said to have used. From the former passage it is evident that baptism had been in use before the coming of Jesus. The Christian church did not invent it, but adopted it. Jesus was baptized, though it is not said that any of the apostles were ever baptized. At any rate the rite was a very simple one in the earliest days of Christianity. It had a very beautiful significance. As water cleanses the body, and keeps us in health, and without it we could not live, it was regarded as a fitting symbol of the action of truth in cleansing the mind, and producing mental well-being. All must be familiar with such expressions as, " Sanctify them through thy truth; thy word is truth." " Now ye are clean through the word which I have spoken unto you." But, in later times baptism became a very elaborate rite; and Professor Lindsay in the *Encyclopaedia Britannica,* after describing some of these ceremonies, says: " It could easily be shown that a great deal of this complex ceremonial took its origin from the introduction of Pagan ceremonies into the Christian worship." H. P. Blavatsky shows how the Romish church has borrowed extensively from Paganism, without always making acknowledgment.

Among the ancients one form of purification was symbolized by the use of water, and another by fire. In *Isis Unveiled,* vol. i, p. 519, we read concerning the great pyramid:

Internally, it was a majestic fane, in whose somber recesses were performed the Mysteries, and whose walls had often witnessed the initiation scenes of members of the royal family. The porphyry sarcophagus, which Professor Piazzi Smyth, Astronomer Royal of Scotland, degrades into a corn-bin, was the *baptismal font,* upon emerging from which, the neophyte was "born again," and became an *adept.*

According to Apuleius, cleansing by water always preceded initiation into the Egyptian and Eleusinian Mysteries. Among the Jews, converts were admitted only after purification by water, to signify that they were cleansed of all their sins. Fire and water were sometimes combined. Ovid (*Fasti iv,* 727) says, " Often, in truth, have I leaped over the fires placed in three rows, and the dripping bough of laurel has flung the sprinkled waters." Dionysius tells us that Romulus, while building the city of Rome had fires kindled and made his people jump through them for purposes of purification or expiation. Payne Knight says that among the Hindûs, Irish, and Phoenicians, passing through the fire was a well-known ceremony. In *The Secret Doctrine,* vol. II, p. 566, *note,* we read that,

In the Cycle of Initiation, which was very long, water represented the first and lower steps toward purification, while trials connected with *fire* came last. Water could regenerate the body of matter; FIRE alone, that of the *inner* Spiritual man.

In *Isis Unveiled,* vol. II, pp. 134, 138, it is said that,

Baptism is one of the oldest rites and was practised by all the nations in their Mysteries, as sacred ablutions. . . . . In the Mithraic sacrifices, during the initiation, a preliminary scene of death was simulated by the neophyte, and it preceded the scene showing him himself "being born again by the rite *of baptism."*

And again, we are told that the Brâhman priest, in order to wash the images of the Gods from the sins of the people, plunges them three times into the water in the name of the mystic trinity. This is very suggestive of the Romanist ritual, in which, as we have seen, there is a threefold application of water, in the name of the Trinity. In the time of Tertullian baptism was well known to be an ancient rite. In reference to the worship of Isis, he says: "In certain sacred rites of the heathen, the mode of initiation is by baptism." And in his day there were some who protested against water-baptism as being opposed to the spirituality of Jesus' religion, and a revival of heathenish and Jewish customs. But these early Quakers were rebuked by the Fathers in the choice language often adopted by early religious controversialists, and were called *serpents,* for, says Tertullian: "vipers, asps, and king serpents themselves mostly look after places that are dry and without water." (Bonwick, *Egyptian Belief and Modern Thought.*)

The rite of baptism seems to have been practised in all the great countries of the world. The dogmatic teachings in regard to it are evidently not derived from the teaching or practice of Jesus, or his immediate disciples, but are in part a transference of ancient ceremonies used when adults were being admitted into the Mysteries. It is but fair to say that most of the Protestant Churches regard baptism as coming in the room of the Old Testament rite by which the children of the Jews were, on the eighth day, admitted into the Jewish Church; and, except for the use of water, they also abjure all forms and dogmas

in connexion with baptism. Among Protest-
ants, baptism and the Eucharist, or Lord's
Supper, are the only recognized sacraments;
.because it is held that a *Christian* Sacrament
must be an ordinance instituted by *Christ himself*. At the same time it is acknowledged that
baptism existed before the time of Jesus, just
as the Passover existed before the Lord's Supper. It is held, however, that Jesus gave a
new significance and power by his command
to observe these two rites.

V

THE "LORD'S SUPPER"

ABOUT no point, not even about baptism has the conflict been waged more fiercely than over the meaning of the Eucharist. The four places in the New Testament where the institution of the Lord's Supper is mentioned are Matt. xxvi, Mark xiv, Luke xxii, and I Cor. xi, and they substantially agree. The account is, that after a meal with his disciples on the night before the betrayal, Jesus instituted an ordinance which the disciples were to observe in his memory. It is said that in doing so,

as they were eating, Jesus took a loaf, and blessed, and brake it; and he gave to the disciples, and said, Take, eat, this is my body. And he took the cup and gave *thanks* (hence the term Eucharist), and gave to them, saying, Drink ye all of it; for this is my blood of the covenant which is shed for many unto remission of sins. (Matt. xxvi.)

St. Paul, whose account may be the earliest, mentions only one giving of thanks, that before breaking the bread. The phrase, "unto remission of sins," is peculiar to the gospel of Matthew. From the four accounts it is evident that Jesus used the bread and wine to represent himself,. his body and blood, and that the disciples were to keep the rite in his memory. Out of this simple ordinance the most astounding dogmas have grown. What was intended by Jesus to help towards a real unity, or *communion*, or brotherhood, has become "a stone of stumbling"; and an occasion of foolish pretension, and uncharitableness. St. Paul, too, dwelt on the idea that the Christ-spirit should be realized as the One Life in all disciples; just as in a family all partake of the same physical food, and have bodily nourishment. Very soon, however, something of a magical influence was ascribed to the bread and wine after having been blessed by the priest. And, in an early canon (xviii, *Nicaea*) we find that deacons must not give the bread and wine to priests, but receive it from them; also the deacons must not sit on the same row of seats with the priests! Alas! for the true spirit of communion, or brotherhood. This striving for front seats has had much to do with the delay of the coming of the Christos. How different this from the spirit of Christ! How different is this canon of the council of bishops from the teaching of Theosophy, " Step out from sunlight into shade to make more room for others."

The doctrine of transubstantiation is the name given to this dogma promulgated by the Roman church concerning the Lord's Supper. According to this dogma, after the priest blesses the bread and wine they are changed into the " body, blood, soul, and divinity of Christ," and they have a magical effect upon the recipient. It is not maintained that the *qualities* of the bread and wine are changed, but it is held that their *essence* is changed. That is to say, no priest would take the bread and wine if he knew that some person had put poison in them. Though the priest declares that his blessing changes the *essence* of

the bread and wine into the essence of Christ
he does not pretend that it alters the *qualities,*
or phenomena! For it could be too easily
proved that it does not.

Luther held that while there was no change
of essence, yet there was a real presence of
Christ *together with* the bread and wine. This
dogma is called *consubstantiation,* and it is the
view held by the Lutheran church. Zwingli
regarded the Eucharist as mainly a commemorative act. Calvin held something of a middle
position between Luther and Zwingli. The
" Confession of Faith " made at Westminster,
and established by acts of Parliament in 1649
and 1690, declared very clearly that the Lord's
Supper was not to be regarded as a "sacrifice,"
but only commemorative of Christ and what
he had done. It also declared that in this
sacrament there was no change either in essence (substance) or qualities; and that the
true partaking of it was a spiritual realizing
of Christ in the heart of the believer. It is
important to notice the teachings regarding
the Eucharist because it is a very vital ques-

tion in connexion with the Reformation in England, and it is coming up at the present time. In a work on the *History of Ritualism* recently published, it is maintained that while the struggle between Henry VIII and the Pope was mainly over the question as to who was ruler in England, yet the deeper cause of division between the Reformers and the Romanists was the so-called " Sacrifice of the Mass." In an extant letter from Pole, the Pope's Legate, this is clearly stated. Latimer declared that he had " read the New Testament over seven times, yet could not find the mass in it." The word " mass," by the way, had no essential connexion with the Eucharist, but is a (presumed) contraction of " *Ite, missa est,*" the words of dismissal to the congregation. It is a term entirely inappropriate as applied to the ceremony of the Eucharist and it cannot be traced back beyond the time of Ambrose.

While the Eucharist is said to be traced back to Jesus, like many other Christian rites and dogmas it finds close parallels in the religious customs of ancient times. In *Isis Unveiled*, vol. II, pp. 43, 44, we read:

Nor does the Mystery of the Eucharist pertain to Christians alone. Godfrey Higgins proves that it was instituted many hundreds of years before the " Paschal Supper," and says that " the sacrifice of bread and wine was common to many ancient nations." Cicero mentions it in his works and wonders at the strangeness of the rite. There had been an esoteric meaning attached to it from the first establishment of the Mysteries, and the *Eucharistia* is one of the oldest rites of antiquity. With the hierophants it had nearly the same significance as with the Christians. Ceres was *bread*, and Bacchus was *wine;* the former meaning regeneration of life from the seed, and the latter — the grape — the emblem of wisdom and knowledge; the accumulation of the spirit of things, and the fermentation and subsequent strength of that esoteric knowledge being justly symbolized by wine.

Froude is said to have written in 1891 to Professor Johnson, author of *Antiqua Mater*, saying: " I have long been convinced that the Christian Eucharist is but a continuation of the Eleusinian Mysteries. St. Paul, in using the word *teleiois* (I Cor. ii, 6) confirms this."

And he (Froude) refers to the words in Cicero, *De Natura Deorum* (xvi) : "although bread is called Ceres and wine Liber, no one can be so foolish as to imagine he eats and drinks God." Bonwick (*Egyptian Belief*, p. 417 *et seq.*) says that the Egyptians declared the bread after the sacerdotal rites to be mystically the body of Isis and Osiris. The cakes were round and were placed on the altar. He quotes Gliddon and Melville as saying that they were "identical in shape with the consecrated cake of the Roman Catholic and Eastern churches," and that "the Egyptians marked the holy bread with St. Andrew's cross." Bonwick adds, that

The *Presence* bread was broken before being distributed by the priests to the people, and was supposed to become the flesh and blood of the Deity. The miracle was wrought by the hand of the officiating priest, who blessed the food. Singularly enough, the mark of that action is still to be seen in specimens remaining in Egypt; for Rougé tells us, "The bread offerings bear the *imprint of the fingers*, the mark of consecration."

In Egypt, as in Rome, the bread was given

to the people, but not the wine. In this the difference between the words of Jesus in the New Testament, and the Egypto-Romanist rite is very marked. The Persians had a similar rite in which a solid and a liquid were used. In the Dionysiac cult wine was used to represent the life of the world. Justin Martyr speaking of the Eucharist says:

In imitation of which the Devil did the like in the Mysteries of Mithras, for you either know or may know that they take bread and a cup of water in the sacrifices of those that are initiated, and *pronounce certain words over it.* (*Ibid.*)

In regard to the rites of Mithras it may not be out of place to quote the words of such a learned Orientalist as Renan (*Hibbert Lecture* 1880, p. 35 *et seq.*). He says:

In the second and third centuries Mithraic worship attained an extraordinary prevalence. I sometimes permit myself to say that if Christianity had not carried the day, Mithraicism would have become the religion of the world. It had its mysterious meetings; its chapels, which bore a strong resemblance to little churches. It forged a very lasting bond of brotherhood between its initiates: it had a Eucharist, a Supper so like the Christian Mysteries, that good Justin Martyr, the Apologist, can find only one explanation of the apparent identity, namely, that Satan, in order to deceive the human race, determined to imitate the Christian ceremonies, and so stole them. A Mithraic sepulcher in the Roman Catacombs is as edifying, and presents as elevated a mysticism as the Christian tombs.

King, in his work on *The Gnostics and Their Remains*, p. 126, says:

The worship of Mithras long kept its ground under Christian Emperors in the capital itself, and doubtless survived its overthrow there for many generations longer in the remote and then semi-independent provinces.

The point of chief interest in comparing Romanist ritual and dogma with those of pre-Christian times, is not simply the fact that the primitive simplicity of Jesus is lost in the picture composed of colors borrowed from ancient religions; but the chief interest is found in the fact that in the course of time those ancient rites and symbols became darkened with superstition and enthralment. Liberation can only come through men waking to the light of Truth; in that light they can, if they will, walk forth as freed men. As the light of the New Age, upon which we have now entered, becomes greater and greater it will be impossible for humanity to sit in darkness, and in the shadow of death. It will feel shame for having crouched so long beneath the reign of dogmatic forms. The study of comparative religion, and the gradual turning over, by archaeology, of the leaves of a forgotten past; the general advance of thought on many lines; and last, but not least, the fuller revelation of the Ancient Wisdom-Religion, given in Theosophy, is making it impossible for the old dogmas to retain their dogmatic influence much longer. The sunlight still floods the land, though we may shut our windows. We do not change things by hiding our heads in the sand.

VI

THE TRINITY

THE dogma of the Trinity is another of those dogmas which is older than Christianity. But here, perhaps, less than anywhere else can Christianity be said to spring from ordinary Judaism. The Divine Unity — " Hear, O Israel, the Lord our God is One " — sounds from every synagogue. The Jews before the Captivity were given to various forms of idolatry, but their conception of the Most High as a Unity, not as a Trinity, marks Jewish thought from first to last. In other words, they kept the First Commandment, even when they did not keep the Second. And yet the esoteric teaching with them was wonderfully like the esoteric teaching of other ancient peoples. Franck, writing of the *Sepher Jetzirah*, says:

The last word of this system is the substitution

of absolute divine Unity for every idea of Dualism, for that pagan philosophy which saw in matter an eternal substance whose laws were not in accord with the Divine Will . . . in fact, in the *Sepher Jetzirah,* God, considered as the Infinite, and consequently indefinable Being extended throughout all things by his power and existence, is while above, yet not outside of numbers, sounds, and letters — the principles and general laws which we recognize.

In the *Kabbalah* we have Unity as the highest conception of the Illimitable One:

In Him is an illimitable abyss of glory, and from it there goeth forth one little spark which maketh the glory of the sun, and of the moon, and of the stars. (Mathers, *Kabbalah Unveiled,* p. 19.)

The Illimitable One exists as a Trinity in the veils of the first three Sephiroth. From this proceeds the *Intellectual world,* considered as a trinity: *Kether,* the crown, *Binah,* intelligence, and *Chokmah,* wisdom. In fact the esoteric teaching in the *Kabbalah* and that found in Eastern philosophy very closely correspond. This may be seen at a glance in *Isis Unveiled,* vol. ii, p. 264. But, for the ordinary Jewish thinker the Divine Unity, or

Monotheism, has been the chief, if not the only teaching.

The success of Mohammedanism is due in no small degree to its theological definiteness, and its simplicity: " There is no God but Allah and Mohammed is his prophet." We might sum up Judaism in similar words: God is One and Moses is his prophet.

The Divine Unity, and the Divine manifested as a Trinity are equally true, and both may be traced to the Ancient Wisdom-Religion. But the modern anthropomorphic Trinity is a very degenerate fiction which later ages have fashioned and worshiped. Some theologians have tried, without much success, to show that there is a great difference between a triad and a trinity; the former, of course, being the oriental, and the later the ecclesiastical term, and concept. The ordinary dogma concerning the Trinity is to this effect: Father, Son, and Holy Ghost are not three Gods, but only one God, yet each is God. They are three, and yet only one. They exist as three persons. It should be noted that the term *" person "* as employed here is claimed to be not the "*persona*" from which the word was originally derived. The ordinary conception of personality implies limitation, but the theologian does not admit that the Persons of the Trinity are finite. Nor are they merely "*aspects*," though that certainly comes nearer it than any other term that can be employed. In truth, when we try to describe, in words of human language, the Infinite, we must very soon become aware of their inadequacy. Our words are born of finite ideas, and are often closely allied to material things, therefore it is impossible that they should suffice to define, describe, or denote the Illimitable, the Absolute. Even our word *spirit* refers originally to the "breath," and the terms "Infinite," and "Absolute" are simply negative terms. "Most High" carries with it the conception of higher and lower and we know that such ideas cannot apply to Deity. Every term in language must be more or less anthropomorphic; but there is a very low form of anthropomorphic conception popularly in use in regard to the

Trinity. The first person of the Trinity is
stern, and is looked upon as a judge; the Son
is merciful; the third person of the Trinity
is less capable of being expressed in human
language, therefore ordinary conceptions are
much more vague, much less definite about the
Holy Ghost than about the Father and the
Son. These very narrow and imperfect conceptions of God might be regarded as comparatively harmless, were it not that such
frightful dogmas have been built upon them.
The common orthodox theology is fabricated
out of misunderstood esoteric teaching. Indeed all metaphysical teachings must be more
or less misunderstood by the mass of mankind.
Few now regard Adam and Eve as the progenitors óf humanity 6000 years ago. The
idea of a garden in which trees of knowledge,
and óf life, grow, is seen to be allegorical.
The " Fall," as taught by orthodoxy, never
existed except in theological imagination, and
it is only a travesty of the true, ancient teaching. The fall was the descent of spirit, of
the Sons of Light, into matter; and it was

part of the great evolutionary process, leading from good to better, best.

But even theologians themselves have not always been of the same mind in explaining the functions of the Trinity. For about 1000 years it was the orthodox teaching that Christ by his death paid the Devil in order that man might be thus redeemed, or bought back. Man, it was held, had sold himself to the Devil; and even the Devil must not be cheated! From the time of Anselm onward the "improved".explanation was that Christ paid the penalty to God the Father, seeing that man by his sin had become the prisoner of divine justice. It was the old Roman law (*lex*) idea, of God as a judge, again becoming prominent. Justice had to be satisfied. Man had sinned against the INFINITE, and that was held to be an *infinite transgression* — therefore no amount of suffering on man's part could exhaust it, man being finite. Karmic retribution was held to be inadequate. Spurgeon and others held that sin could not exhaust itself: "Man sinned while he suffered, therefore by the very nature and necessity of the case, sin was an eternal evil; eternity could not exhaust it." Man could only be saved by an *infinite* sufferer in his stead, *i. e.,* by Christ. Against this, many of the more liberal theologians held that a *finite creature* (man) could not commit an *infinite sin.*

The whole theological conception is a miserable nightmare of ages of darkness. Truly man makes his God in his own image; and the supposed relationship of the persons of the Trinity to each other, and to man, is very much on the level of the ordinary law court. It is often said that Christ came to reveal God to man as the heavenly Father; but in a very few centuries the churches, saturated with the legal and materialistic spirit of Rome, made a trinity in which the first person is an implacable judge who must have full payment even though the innocent should suffer for the guilty.

Now, this dogma of the Trinity, this unworthy conception of the Eternal, truly belongs to the outer court. What then is the

truth, the inner teaching, of which the ordinary theological dogma is such a perversion?
It is a fact that on the great stairway of the
Universe the higher helps the lower. The soul
must descend into matter to fulfil the great
cycle of evolution, of the Great Breath. The
Great Helpers may be truly said to lay their
lives down as a pathway for weaker lives. As
the sun gives light and life to the planets, so
in like manner does the divine principle run
through all from the highest down to man and
beyond. It is in a sense suffering for others;
but it is that of the mother for her child; that.
of the teacher for his pupil; not that of a
guilty person going free by casting his sins
on someone else.

The Eastern conception of the One Life
manifesting itself under the threefold aspects
of Brahmâ, Vishnu, and S'iva, has probably
become nearly as much materialized in India
as the corresponding dogma has in Western
lands. The right conception can be reached
only by seeking the primitive teaching, the
shrine, not the *pronaos*. To study the septen-

ary constitution of man is the best way to get a true conception of what is above man: above, and yet in man; for we are even now temples of God, and the Holy Ghost dwells in us, as the Christian scripture says.

This is the ancient teaching which is needed to give wisdom to man. To realize that there is in us the potency of all the planes of the universe, while, at the same time we feel, " not as though we had already attained," this is to have true humility and sublime hope. " For *now* are we the Sons of God, but it doth not yet appear what we shall be." Man has within him the Holy of Holies, the Spark of the One Flame. To lift the lower nature into closer and closer union, or harmony with this Central Shrine is to live in harmony with the Soul and movement of the universe. Nothing can prevent the perfect justice, or Karma, of the man of sin within us reaping what he has sown; but by the union of the lower nature with the Christ in us a mighty change of relation is brought about. As this is studied and realized by men generally the crudities of ecclesiasticism, and all the ecclesiastical fabrication and manipulation of sacraments to secure heaven will vanish like the shapes of darkness before the rising sun. Much of it has already vanished. And every few years the world of thinking people is bursting through dogma after dogma, as the growing tree casts its bark.

VII

THE DEVIL AND ATONEMENT

NEXT to the Trinity the most important dogma to be found in ecclesiasticism is concerning the Devil. Many have maintained that without the Devil the church could not exist. It is one of the saddest aspects of our lower human nature that in the East and West alike such horrible pictures of devils and hells should have been invented. Happily this dogma is no longer accepted by intelligent men; though not a few among the ignorant and superstitious are still in the bondage of fear. No doubt there may be a certain loosening of restraint as the old terrors pass away, and the lower selfish nature has not yet come under the control and impulse of the soul within. No doubt men who have been terrorized into morality by fear of the Devil, or hell, will not all at once learn to hate evil in itself and avoid it, and to do good for the love of it; but true morality is in the motive, and fear is an infinitely lower motive than love.

Closely connected with the dogmas of the Trinity and of the Devil, is that of the atonement, which we have touched upon already. The true at-one-ment is the transforming of the lower nature into the image of the Christos within. This is the real alchemy, the change of the lead of the lower man into the pure gold of the higher. Of all miracles, or wonders, this is the greatest; compared with it the transmutation of physical substances would be trivial. But dogmatic teaching has completely changed this great fact of nature into a legal or mercantile transaction. By the " propitiatory sacrifice " of Christ, as it is called, God is said to be reconciled to man, or as others put it, man is reconciled unto God. The ancient and true teaching is that a great vital change takes place in man, in harmony with Cosmic Law, or the Life of the Universe. The inmost of man is indeed the secret place of the Most High. The lower

nature of man corresponds to the *pronaos* of
the temple. Instead of this, orthodox dogma
makes God a something outside of man, who
must be propitiated for Adam's offense in the
Garden of Eden. Instead of the return of
the prodigal son which Christ pictures; instead of the great Cosmic process of return
to the Divine, of which the change in man is
a clear type and illustration, dogmatic theology
gives us the noisy machinery of a law-court.
For the heavenly Father revealed by Jesus
we have the Roman magistrate. And man,
instead of being a Son of God, as the Bible
says, is declared by the church to be the child
of the Devil. Salvation is made a legal or
mechanical thing, for the supposed magical
power of the properly ordained priest is said
to drive out the Devil and introduce the Divine
Spirit. There is still need for Jesus to say,
" the flesh profiteth nothing; the words that
I speak unto you they are spirit, and they are
life."

It may easily be seen that the whole vast
structure of dogma is like an inverted pyramid.

For if the story of Adam and Eve be allegorical teaching about primitive man before he had a coat of skin (that is, a *physical* body) then how baseless are all the dogmas which have been reared upon this allegory read as a literal fact! History is the great drama of the soul. There is no such thing as *profane* history; all is the shadow of the Divine. The Incarnation is the very life of the Universe, and true on all planes. It is the in-dwelling of the Christ, or Christos, " Christ *in you* the hope of glory," as the apostle says.

VIII

DIVINE INCARNATIONS

AS part of the great " Redemption," or " Return," it has been the ancient teaching that in times of great need in the life of humanity, at certain cyclic periods, a lofty embodiment of the Divine takes place. Thus, in the *Bhagavad Gîtâ*, ch. iv, Krishna says:

I produce myself among creatures, O son of Bhârata, whenever there is a decline of virtue and an insurrection of vice and injustice in the world; and thus I incarnate from age to age for the preservation of the just, the destruction of the wicked, and the establishment of righteousness.

It is this great world-fact that helps us to understand the wonderful resemblances recorded concerning the Great Teachers throughout the ages. It is well known that the idea of the Logos was common to Egyptians, Hindûs, Persians, Chaldaeans, and other nations.

From what source except the great Wisdom-
Religion could these different nations have
obtained it? Among the Egyptians Thoth is
called the Word, or Logos. " I know the
mystery of the Divine Word," is the translation of the characters found on a stele in the
Louvre. Lenormant speaks of the doctrine of
the Logos as being almost universal. Bonwick says: " The Incarnation idea is well
illustrated in Egyptian theology. It is not the
vulgar, coarse and sensual story as in Greek
mythology, but refined, moral, and spiritual."
(*op. cit.* p. 406.) And in this connexion the
author of the Tract Society's work on Egypt
writes :

This most ancient theology, taught to the initiated
and concealed from the vulgar, that God created all
things at first by the primary emanation from Himself, his first-born, who was the author and giver
of all wisdom and all knowledge in heaven and in
earth, being at the same time the Wisdom and the
Word of God.

According to Mr. Sharpe, the Egyptologist,
the whole idea of the incarnation and birth by

a virgin is depicted on the wall of a temple at Thebes. Gerald Massey in his *Egyptian Exodus*, has these words:

> We shall see the good Osiris, and his Son the Word made true,
> Who died and rose — the Karast! — in the Aah-en-Ru.
> He who daily dies to save us, passing Earth and Hades through;
> Lays his life down for a pathway to the Aah-en-Ru.

Among the Assyrians the Logos was known as the *Marduk*. He was the eldest Son of Hea; and was named the merciful one. In Kitto's *Biblical Cyclopaedia* we read concerning the Logos:

> This mysterious doctrine of Emanation is at once the most universal and the most memorable of traditions; so universal, that traces of it may be found throughout the whole world; so ancient, that its source is hidden in the grey mists of antiquity.

It must be acknowledged by every impartial student of the history of comparative religion that the dogmas of all religions represent a very materialistic, and a very inadequate conception of the One Life and Its manifestations. But, notwithstanding the great changes and obscurations produced by dogmatic theology, there is generally some point or points which serve as a connecting link between the Ancient Wisdom-Religion and the ecclesiastical dogmas of today. We have seen how unworthy are the modern anthropomorphic conceptions of the Eternal. Man has made his God in his own image truly, not according to the glory of the inner sanctuary, but after the likeness of the outer court, the lower human mind. And mankind as a whole must suffer on account of these false conceptions of the Highest.

IX

"ORIGINAL SIN" AND PERFECTION

THERE is another matter of vital importance — man's idea of his own nature;
and in regard to this the church dogmas have
exerted a most baleful influence. The doctrine
of innate human depravity, or of original sin,
has settled like a dark cloud over a large part
of the human race. The true, celestial origin
of the real Self was lost sight of in the course
of ages, and man's conception of himself became more and more confined to, and identified with the body and the lower mind. Hence
it is that in the Old Testament we find very
little said about the real nature of man. The
true knowledge was no doubt concealed in
symbols and in ritual; but, for the mass of
the people, the Old Testament scriptures teach
little about the hereafter. In the New Testament the consciousness of immortality becomes

clearer; but even in the writings of St. Paul we do not find a very distinct teaching as to the nature of man. So much is this the case that scholars maintain that the threefold nature of man as spirit, soul, and body, cannot be very clearly deduced from the New Testament use of these words in one or two places, soul and spirit being often used interchangeably. So it came to be the common notion that man was a body possessing a soul, instead of man realizing that he *is a soul,* and that the body is only a temporary covering — an outer coat — and no part of the real man at all. It thus remained for the scientific materialists of the present day to discover that man is only a collection of atoms, some of whose functions are called mind! Who will deny that mankind has reached the lowest point of the arc of descent into matter? The materialist is a monist, but to him matter is the one and only thing, and not spirit. And yet St. Paul had said plainly that there is a natural body and that there is a spiritual body. And the image of the grain of wheat which he uses was a

teaching which he either saw, or might have
seen in the Mysteries. The ancient oracle
" Know Thyself," must ever be regarded as
of supreme importance; and, what we know
ourselves to be is the yard-stick by which we
measure all things else.

For popular teaching it is perhaps sufficient
to speak of the higher mind, and the lower
mind; or the carnal man, and the spiritual
man, of St. Paul. Every one is at once conscious of two forces struggling within; a
selfish power, and an unselfish power. This
struggle is the Great War, the Holy War.
But for many thoughtful people the knowledge
of man as septenary, and his correspondence,
therefore, with this septenary universe, as
taught by Theosophy, must prove to be a revelation of the greatest importance. It is not
merely a speculative truth, it has many practical bearings also. As we study ourselves
and get to understand better what we are,
we see more clearly the path to deliverance.
We understand better the tyranny of the lower
nature, whose selfishness has caused 'so much

misery in the world; and we are enabled to reach to the true and harmonious order and relationship of all the principles. This is that state when the Divine Will is done on earth as it is in heaven. This is the real meaning of the "coming of the Kingdom." We may be perfectly certain that nothing can be more hurtful to man than this low and erroneous idea of human nature which dogmatic teaching has foisted upon the world for nearly two thousand years. On the other hand, the true conception of man's sevenfold nature, and the realization of his inherent divinity, must prove a source of light, hope, and strength. Being conscious of the Christos as our *real Self* within, we must feel that "upward calling" of which the initiate apostle speaks.

Dogmatic theology as expressed in creeds may be likened to a hard shell which prevents the germ inside from expanding. There is a germ of truth which may be traced to very ancient times, but this germ, instead of being allowed to expand and become a tree of wisdom, is imprisoned through the ages. The whole system by which creeds have been made and perpetuated is entirely hurtful to man's inner nature. In the first place, from a very small beginning, a vast and complicated statement is concocted through much debate, passion, and conflict. The decision, of perhaps a bare majority of men, prompted in some instances by spite against some person, is the foundation of a creed, or some part of a creed. And even were the elements of passion and prejudice absent: even if absolute unanimity existed among those making the creed, there is no reason why their opinions should become a binding law upon future generations, making progress difficult or impossible. In the very nature of things men's minds should expand, their views widen; therefore, there should be a revision of creeds periodically. Even the best statement of beliefs must be regarded as tentative. Instead of this, we find that by a majority vote of not very learned or impartial men, in a semi-barbarous age, a dogma is fastened round the neck of future ages of progress and enlightenment. It is then regarded as heresy to attempt to amend the creed; which, though it may be called the "subordinate standard," becomes virtually the only, and infallible standard and authority. But this is not the whole of the mischief. Every charitable person who endows a church holding such or such a creed is making creed-revision more and more impossible. It is a well-known fact that trust-deeds have more than once tied the hands of reformers. The celebrated case of the Free Church of Scotland is a case in point. There, the whole body of the church, almost (1100 churches out of 1128), voted to join with a sister church, the United Presbyterian, holding the same creed; but the minority of 28 held out on some small points of church government, and eventually got a decision in its favor by the House of Lords. The result was world-wide consternation, for if the highest legal authority in England was right, the effects would be very far-reaching. It required a special Act of Parliament to settle matters on any sort of logical basis, and even then, so it is reported, the 28 ministers and churches of the minority got all they could reasonably use of the total property, which had amounted to many millions, in colleges, schools, etc. in Scotland, India, and elsewhere. May be there was some working of Karma in this for the action of the Madras people to H. P. Blavatsky in 1884.

With the best of motives those endowing creeds, and the like, may be doing much mischief to posterity. And it is difficult to know how to improve matters permanently in this respect. For, it is clearly a good thing to assist with money, or the like, a form of teaching which a man believes to be true. In connexion with this the general law should be kept in mind, the more particular the creed, the less is its extension. The shorter and more general the creed, then the greater its extension, or the greater number of minds that can accept it. But the radical difficulty arises out of the nature of the lower mind itself. It should be possible for men to unite on a *love of what is good and true,* rather than on the basis that they will all agree as to certain dogmas. As a step to this, the creeds should be laid on the shelf — and kept there — as historical documents; interesting relics of an out-lived past, along with the thumb-screws and other mementoes of "the good old times." Religion should be a healer and unifier, but dogmatic religion has been a prolific source of strife in all lands, and in all ages. And often, the smaller the points of dispute, the more fiercely has the war of sects raged.

In this age, the Ancient Wisdom-Religion, Theosophy, comes to point the disputants to the source, the one source, from which religions and philosophies as well as races and nations have sprung. The dogmatic teachings have obscured and perverted the truth, and produced lack of unity and then strife, among men who should be living together as brethren. At first, many do not like this. Each person and each sect claims a higher position than others. The very name of Comparative Religion has been hateful to narrow-minded people. Nevertheless, the process of light-bringing goes on, and even those churches which are the last to progress have advanced a little; though, if one may judge by the public utterances of some, the tendency is to go backward rather than forward. A recent telegram states that the Professor of a celebrated British University declared that the cure for the present unrest in religious matters would be a return to Calvinism! Many have not advanced much from that position, therefore the return would not be a long journey.

X

THE SEAT OF AUTHORITY

THERE are two other dogmas which deserve mention — the plenary inspiration of the Bible, and Papal infallibility — though neither can be said to spring from the Ancient Wisdom-Religion.

As to the dogma of Papal Infallibility, while it does not directly concern any church except the Roman, yet we find in other denominations something of the same tendency to make someone, or something, a standard by which to measure right and wrong. It is an infallible book, or an infallible creed, if not an infallible pope. The absurdity of regarding any person as infallible, even when speaking *ex cathedra,* is too evident, even from the history of the Roman church itself, to deserve serious attention. It finds its reason of existence only from the fact that very many people wish some one

else to think for them, on religious matters at
any rate. But, however useful external helps
may be, the primary authority is the conscience, the voice of the God within; as
Dr. Martineau has clearly shown in his well-
known work, *The Seat of Authority in Religion.*
Indeed the most servile worshiper of external
authority must, at least once in his life, exercise the privilege of judgment, when he abdi-
cates to another his own right to judge in
matters of religion. The true cure for this
folly is to understand the real nature of man,
as made known in Theosophy, and to respond
to the voice of the Christos within — that voice
which comes from the inner shrine of the
human soul. The same applies to a book
supposed to be infallible. The different
parts composing this book had, at one time or
other, to be examined and judged by men
no better than ourselves, as to whether or not
they should be made part of the canon of
scripture. The judgment, the conscience, had
to be used to decide in the first instance what
writings should be regarded as the Bible.

Sometimes one book was rejected, sometimes another was rejected. And as Reuss has shown in his history of the Canon, its formation has been the result of a gradual growth, and not accomplished in a little while, as many suppose.

Then, as to the question of inspiration, while it is a self-evident fact that certain scriptures carry with them the evidence of a lofty source, it is quite a different thing to declare that all the words of the Old and New Testaments are God-inspired. This is the doctrine of plenary inspiration — an infallible book — and it is based specially on II Timothy, iii, 16, " all scripture is given by inspiration of God " etc. The Revised Version more correctly renders it, " every scripture inspired of God is also profitable," etc., which conveys a very different meaning from that commonly given to it.

The question of " what is Inspiration? " cannot be discussed here; but the general principle may be noted, that every channel through which light comes has a modifying influence on it. This is true in the spiritual as it is in the material world. Human thought, human language, individual peculiarities — all these stamp themselves on any message, even if given from the highest source. Then, as to the transmission of this scripture, all we can venture is to hope and believe that it is substantially as first given. Absolute infallibility cannot be entertained for a moment. And, after all, what better criterion can we apply to a writing than that it has met human needs and stood the test of time, that it has become a great classic? The more human the scripture is, the more it is divine. Jesus appealed to his hearers to accept or reject his words on the ground of their inherent truth. We cannot improve on that.

There are other dogmas, such as that of the resurrection of the physical body; the second Advent; the Last Judgment, which are but partial and therefore imperfect conceptions of certain truths, and as such do not occupy the place they once held. Here we are in the tomb of the flesh; at death we drop from us this mortal body, as we put off a garment, and rise into a higher state of existence. This is shown very graphically in an ancient Egyptian picture. Neith, the Divine Mother, is the firmament. The physical body, colored red falls to the ground, but the real man, colored blue, rises up towards heaven. It reminds one of St. Paul where he speaks of the natural body being sown, the spiritual body being raised, in I Cor. xv. The only sense in which we can be said to have a physical resurrection is through Reincarnation. We do stand again on earth in a physical body; and it may have been from this truth that the notion of a bodily resurrection sprang into existence.

H. P. Blavatsky tells us (*The Secret Doctrine,* vol. ii. p. 459) that the *sarcophagus* or tomb in the shrine of the temple was regarded with the greatest veneration. It was "the symbol of *resurrection* cosmic, solar (or diurnal), and human." The sun was the great symbol of this in heaven, man was the symbol on earth. The materialization of this esoteric teaching well illustrates the change from the Crypt or Adytum to the Pronaos.

The " Second Coming " was in the first instance a conception based on the words of Jesus, that some of the generation then living should not taste of death until the coming of the Son of Man. All through the centuries the idea has come to the surface again and again, sometimes producing very extraordinary popular delusions. But there is a real sense in which the Christos, the Christ in man, is coming with power and glory. As the Christos develops in each heart the general manifestation of the Christos in Humanity is drawing nearer, until at last " every eye shall see him." But, before this grand consummation there must be more than one Day of Judgment. Such days of sifting, or separating, come at the close of cycles. The Great Day, or the " Last Day," is when the manifested universe returns into the bosom of the Infinite — The Great Day " BE WITH US," mentioned in *The Secret Doctrine*. This part of the Wisdom-Religion has been narrowed and materialized in the Christian ages, not only by theologians, but even by poets and painters. The *pronaos* here, more than in most other cases, has degraded the teaching of the shrine.

We have now entered upon the New Age. The Ancient Wisdom-Religion is being restored. The horizon of the human mind is being extended, and the light of the Christos is shining. A natural result must be the passing away of dogmas and creeds, and everything else that fetters intellectual growth, and all that "hinders or impedes the action of the nobler will."

The best and surest way to remove false teachings is to show how they arose. The best way to remove animosities is to demonstrate that we are many members in one body, that we have had a common origin, and always have a common interest. This is the mission and aim of the Wisdom-Religion.

It has been the natural tendency of dogma to produce strife in the human family. It has often been the policy, even of those called

Christians, to divide men and nations from each other, so as to rule them more easily. It is time for all this to cease. The command has come to us as it came to Moses: "Speak unto the Children of Israel, THAT THEY GO FORWARD." The bondage of dogmas, the slavery of creeds, and all the darkness of medieval theology we must leave behind us. A more glorious Land of Promise than ever poet dreamed of beckons us onward. The Ancient Wisdom, and the Ancient Teachers are here again. Man is awakening to the consciousness that he is divine, and he hears a divine voice within him — a voice from the Holy of Holies — say: "Arise, shine, for thy Light is come!"

THEOSOPHICAL

MANUALS

XVII

EARTH

ITS PARENTAGE, ITS ROUNDS AND ITS RACES

The Aryan Theosophical Press
Point Loma, California
1911

THEOSOPHICAL MANUALS

XVII

EARTH:

ITS PARENTAGE; ITS ROUNDS AND ITS RACES

BY

A STUDENT

The Aryan Theosophical Press
Point Loma, California
1908

PREFACE

THE remarks under this head are intended
to be introductory to each of the Manuals.
First, as to the spirit in which they are offered. These Manuals are not written in a
controversial spirit, nor as an addition to the
stock of theories awaiting public approval.
The writers have no time to waste in arguing
with people who do not wish to be convinced,
or who ridicule everything which is new to
their limited outlook. Their message is for
those who desire to know — those who are
seeking for something that will solve their
doubts and remove their difficulties. For such,
all that is needed is a clear exposition of the
Theosophical teachings; for they will judge
of the truth of a teaching by its power to answer the questions they ask. People realize,
much more now than in the early days of the
Theosophical Society, the value of Theosophy;

for the ever-increasing difficulties engendered
by selfishness and materialism, by doubt and
the multiplicity of theories, have created an
urgent demand which it alone can satisfy.

Again, it is necessary to state clearly and
emphatically the genuine teachings of Theosophy, as given by the Founder of the Theosophical Society, H. P. Blavatsky, and her
successors, William Q. Judge and Katherine
Tingley. For, as H. P. Blavatsky predicted,
there are persons who have sought to pervert
these teachings and turn them into a source
of profit to themselves and their own selfish
and ambitious schemes. The true teachings
do not lend themselves to such purposes; their
ideals are of the purest and most unselfish.
Hence these persons have sought to promulgate under the name of Theosophy a perverted
form of the teachings, from which Brotherliness and other pure motives are omitted, and
which contains doctrines which H. P. Blavatsky showed to be maleficent and destructive.
As these pseudo-Theosophists have gained a
certain amount of notoriety by using the names
of the Theosophical Society and its Leaders,
it is necessary to warn the public against them

and their misrepresentations. Their teachings
can easily be shown, by comparison, to be directly contrary to those of H. P. Blavatsky,
whom they nevertheless profess to follow. Instead of having for their basis self-sacrifice,
self-purification and the elevation of the human race, these teachings too often pander to
ambition, vanity and curiosity. In many cases
they are altogether ridiculous, and only calculated to make people laugh. Nevertheless,
as these travesties have served to discredit the
name of Theosophy and to keep earnest inquirers away from the truth, it is well that the
public should know their nature and origin.
They are the work of people who were at one
time members of the Theosophical Society,
but who did not find in it that food for their
own personalities of which they were really in
search. So they turned against their teachers
in wounded pride and vanity, and started little
societies of their own — with themselves at
the head.

The writers of these Manuals have no personal grievance against any such calumniators.
Inspired by a profound love of the sublime
teachings of Theosophy, they have made it

their life-work to bring the benefits which they
have thereby received within the reach of as
many people as possible. And they feel that
they will have the hearty sympathy and co-
operation of the public in exposing folly and
bringing the truth to light.

Theosophy strikes unfamiliar ground in
modern civilization, because it does not come
under any particular one of the familiar headings of Religion, Science, Philosophy, etc. into
which our age has divided its speculative activities. It dates back to a period in the history
of mankind when such distinctions did not exist, but there was one Gnosis or Knowledge
embracing all. Religion and Science, as we
have them today, are but imperfect growths
springing from the remnants of that great
ancient system, the Wisdom-Religion, which
included all that we now know as religion and
science, and much more. Hence Theosophy
will not appeal to the same motives as religion
and science. It will not offer any cheap and
easy salvation or put a premium upon mental
inactivity and spiritual selfishness. Neither
can it accomodate itself to the rules laid down
by various schools of modern thought as to

what constitutes proof and what does not. But it can and does appeal to the Reason. The truth of doctrines such as Theosophy maintains, can only be estimated by their ability to solve problems and by their harmony with other truths which we know to be true. But in addition to this we have the testimony of the ages, which has been too long neglected by modern scholarship, but which is now being revealed by archaeologists and scholars, as H. P. Blavatsky prophesied that it would in this century.

It may perhaps be as well also to remind those who would criticise, that the state of modern opinion is scarcely such as to warrant anybody in assuming the attitude of a judge. It would be quite proper for a Theosophist, instead of answering questions or attempting to give proofs, to demand that his questioners should first state their own case, and to be himself the questioner. The result would certainly show that Theosophy, to say the very least, stands on an equal footing with any other view, since there is no certain knowledge, no satisfying explanation, to be found anywhere.

Since the days when the wave of materialism swept over the world, obliterating the
traces of the ancient Wisdom-Religion and
replacing it by theological dogmatism our religions have had nothing to offer us in the way
of a philosophical explanation of the laws of
Being as revealed in Man and in Nature.
Instead we have only had bare statements
and dogmatic assertions. The higher nature
of man is represented by such vague words
as Spirit and Soul, which have little or no
meaning for the majority. The laws of the
universe are briefly summed up under the
term " God," and all further consideration of
them shut off. Then came a reaction against
the dogmatism of religion, and man pinned
his faith to knowledge gained by study and
reflection, limiting his researches however to
the outer world as presented by the senses,
and fearing to trench upon the ground which
dogmatic theology had rendered the field of
so much contention. The result of this has
been that neither in religions nor sciences,
have we any teaching about the higher nature of man or the deeper mysteries of the
universe. This is a field which is left entirely

unexplored, or is at best the subject of tentative and unguided conjectures.

Until, therefore, religious teachers have something definite, consistent, and satisfactory to offer, and until science can give us something better than mere confessions of nescience or impudent denials with regard to everything beyond its own domain, Theosophy can afford to assume the rôle of questioner rather than that of questioned, and does not *owe* anybody any explanations whatever. It is sufficient to state its tenets and let them vindicate themselves by their greater reasonableness; and any further explanation that may be offered is offered rather from goodwill than from any obligation.

Theosophy undertakes to explain that which other systems leave unexplained, and is, on its own special ground, without a competitor. It can issue a challenge to theology, science, and other modern systems, to surpass it in giving a rational explanation of the facts of life.

Again, there are some questions which it is beyond the reach of the human mind, in *its present stage of development,* to answer; and it would scarcely be just to arraign Theosophy for not answering these.

Judgment should in all cases be preceded by careful study. There are always those who will impatiently rush to questions which a further study would have rendered unnecessary; and it is safe to say that the majority of "objections" raised to Theosophical teachings are such as could have been solved by the objector himself, had he been a genuine student. In the ordinary courses of education, scholars are required and are content, to accept provisionally many of the teacher's statements, in full confidence that further study will explain what in the beginning cannot be made clear. In the same spirit an earnest student of Theosophy will be wise enough to hold many of his difficulties in reserve, until, by further investigation, he has gained better acquaintance with his subject. In the case of those who are not willing to adopt these wise and patient methods of study, it may be reasonably questioned whether they are the more anxious to learn or to disprove.

Above all it is sought to make these Man-

uals such that they shall appeal to the heart
and not *merely* to the head; that they shall
be of practical service to the reader in the
problems of his daily life, and not mere intellectual exercises. For there have been in
past days books written by persons more distinguished for a certain grade of mental nim-
bleness than for heartfelt devotion to the
cause of truth; and these have appealed only
to those people who love intricate philosophical problems better than practical work. But
as H. P. Blavatsky so frequently urged, the
message of Theosophy is for suffering humanity; and the great Teachers, whose sole purpose is to bring to mankind the Light of
Truth and the saving grace of real Brotherliness can have no interest in catering for
the mental curiosity of merely a few well-
to-do individuals. Even soulless men, said
H. P. Blavatsky, can be brilliantly intellectual;
but for those who are in earnest in their desire to reach the higher life intellectual fireworks alone will have little attraction. We
intend, therefore, to keep the practical aspect
of the teachings always to the front, and to
show, as far as possible, that they are what

they claim to be — the gospel of a new hope and salvation for humanity.

These Booklets are not all the product of a single pen, but are written by different Students at the International Headquarters of the UNIVERSAL BROTHERHOOD AND THEO- SOPHICAL SOCIETY at Point Loma, California. Each writer has contributed his own quota to the series.

For further explanations on Theosophy generally, the reader is referred to the Book List published elsewhere in this volume and to the other Manuals of this series, which treat of Theosophy and the various Theosophical teachings.

CONTENTS

INTRODUCTORY

THE past history of mankind is one of the most important subjects within the scope of Theosophy, and in its fulness is one of the most difficult to comprehend; for man was not always constituted as he is now, and some of his former experiences are not easy to be realized by the materialistic mind cramped by the idea that intelligence or self-consciousness requires a physical brain and nervous system for its existence. Still the idea is dimly penetrating the most intuitive minds of the age that conscious life in subtle or ethereal forms is possible; it is even suspected that this may become a matter of actual knowledge, and not of faith in some authority. The ·recent advance of science in its bold guess that "solid matter" is merely an "apparent or phenomenal" manifestation of electricity (whatever that may be), has prepared the ground for new ideas about subtler degrees of matter as vehicles of consciousness. As H. P. Blavatsky truly prophesied many years ago, the twentieth century is already providing suitable conditions for the reception and comprehension of the invaluable hints that Theosophy has brought to the world, real " missing links." The break-up of materialism in intellectual spheres of thought and the cautious acknowledgment of the existence of certain kinds of psychic phenomena, such as hypnotism, by educated people, has prepared many to accept as at least possible, facts which were scouted with contumely by the learned ignorance of thirty years ago when H. P. Blavatsky set forth the epoch-making teachings with which she was entrusted, and illustrated them by a few demonstrations of her control of forces behind the veil as yet unknown to science.

But notwithstanding the modern boast that thought is free, it has only been possible for a very small portion of the Secret Doctrine of the ages to be given out by its Custodians, little more, in fact, than a few leading suggestions and pregnant hints for the intuitive; for the world is not ready nor anxious to hear the plain truth. One of H. P. Blavatsky's Teachers said: " Lead the life necessary for the acquisition of such knowledge and powers, and Wisdom will come to you naturally," a course that was none the less necessary in the time of Christ than today: " If any man will do his will he shall know of the doctrine," (John, vii. 17). In *The Secret Doctrine* the following passage occurs, in the course of a full explanation of the origin of the work:

The outline of a few fundamental truths from the Secret Doctrine of the Archaic ages is now permitted to see the light, after long millenniums of the most profound silence and secrecy. I say "a *few* truths" advisedly, because that which must remain unsaid could not be contained in a hundred such volumes, nor could it be imparted to the present generation of Sadducees. But even the little that is now given is better than complete silence upon those vital truths. The world of today . . . has now become a vast arena — a true valley of discord and of eternal strife — a necropolis wherein lie buried the highest and most holy aspirations of our Spirit-Soul . . . but there is a fair minority of earnest students who are entitled to learn the few truths that may be given to them now.

This was written in 1888 and the progress of thought has been sweeping in the Theosophical direction ever since.

H. P. Blavatsky's work *The Secret Doctrine*, from which most of the facts mentioned in this Manual are obtained, contains a mine of suggestions of extraordinary value in clearing up the darkness of the past. *The Secret Doctrine* was written largely to support the funddamental Theosophical principle that man is a divine soul, temporarily obscured by the conditions through which he has to fight in order to obtain higher states of wisdom and perfection; also to prove the existence of a widely extended knowledge of history, natural science, and a more profound understanding of the nature of man, in remotest antiquity, as well as to show that all the ancient religions have a common basis of truth. It also contains much positive teaching, and clear directions about the way to obtain more.

II

DESIGN IN NATURE

WHO does not remember the story of the good fairy that came to the rescue of the distressed maiden who had thousands of feathers to sort in a single night? When the fairy waved her wand, lo! the feathers all flew into their places. Theosophy is the fairy that brings order into the chaos of anthropology, biology and archaeology; it studies the traditions and so-called superstitions preserved orally and in ancient inscriptions and manuscripts such as the Egyptian *Book of the Dead*, the Indian *Purânas*, the American *Popol Vuh*, the Chinese writings, the Hebrew *Pentateuch*, etc., and it proves that the archaic traditions are not mere fairy stories made up by simple innocents, ignorant and credulous, to please other childish minds more credulous than themselves. Theosophy repudiates the materialism of the "animistic" theories, the crude and superficial "phallic-worship" explanation of primitive myths, as well as the popular hypothesis that the time-honored mythologies are nothing but Solar Myths or fanciful renderings of the physical phenomena of outer Nature, on the ground that all or any of these are inadequate to meet the facts as a whole. Theosophy proves that the myths preserve correct traditions of past history and a profound knowledge of the hidden laws of nature, but until H. P. Blavatsky brought the key they remained a sealed book, for they have been so much obscured and distorted by design and erroneous transmission that all the learning and research spent upon them had never revealed the deeper meanings.

To the average man who thinks at all about the circumstances of life, but who has no clue to the meaning, this world is a very curious and barbarous place, and if he really believed it the work of a Personal God, it is no wonder that grave doubts of either the power or the beneficence of such a Deity should arise in his mind. He wonders how he got here, why things are not in better shape, why evil should apparently triumph, and why it is easier for mankind to sink below the normal than to rise above it in so many cases; in short, what the real object of the conflict of life can be. The world of intelligence has almost outgrown the theological idea that a Personal and Anthropomorphic God made everything — including Eternal Damnation for the majority, the unbelievers — for his own good pleasure, "for His own glory," — unless, of course, that is taken in a profoundly mystical sense — and yet people generally take such short views of life that existence seems meaningless and inconsequential; they live on, as far as they know, because there is really nothing better to do, and so they continue to chase the ever-elusive mirage called "pleasure" and to dread a change of conditions which might mean the falling out of the frying-pan into the fire.

Theosophy turns for us the first key of knowledge, and renders our greater and lesser lives comprehensible as a whole, as parts of an

intelligently ordered, progressive and righteous
Plan. But the existence of a plan does not
imply a Personal Anthropomorphic Designer,
separate from the work, " made in the image of
man." The Theosophical concept of Divinity
is far too high to admit of limitations, and to
speculate upon the nature of the Absolute is
as profitless as it is blasphemous to attach
human attributes to That which is immeasur-
ably removed from the grasp of brain-mind
thought. The Bible says darkness is around
His pavilion, and Manu, the prehistoric Indian
lawgiver speaks of " Him who exists by himself, whom the spirit alone can perceive, who
is imperceptible to the organs of sense, who is
without visible parts, eternal, the soul of all
beings and whom none can comprehend." Luther writes: " God is indivisible and indefinable; what we can define or see is not God.
Men desire in their speculations to apprehend
God; they apprehend in his place — the Devil,
who would also pose as God."

But as the " Spirit of God," the active principle, " moves upon the face of the waters,"

i. e., as the Divine Thought takes form, the Universe begins to manifest the Kosmic Plan inherent in the very nature of things, for the Triangle of Spirit, Matter, and Energy is One in essence.

> Before beginning and without an end,
> As space eternal and as surety sure,
> Is fixed a Power Divine which moves to good,
>   Only its laws endure.
> It maketh and unmaketh, mending all;
> What it hath wrought is better than hath been,
> Slow grows the splendid pattern that it plans
>   Its wistful hands between.
> Such is the law which moves to righteousness,
> Which none at last can turn aside or stay;
> The heart of it is Love, the end of it
>   Is Peace and Consummation sweet. Obey!
>   *Light of Asia*

H. P. Blavatsky speaks of Compassion as the one indestructible characteristic of all manifestations of Deity, and Theosophy does not sentimentally teach universal brotherhood as a pretty theory of human invention, nor as a mere pious aspiration of what might be, but as a fact firmly rooted in the very nature of

things; and even the comparatively limited
portion of the Theosophical philosophy yet
brought to the attention of the West supplies
enough material to prove that a rational order
exists in Nature, and that there is a real evolution, *i. e.*, an Evolution or Unfolding of the
inner powers of the immortal " thread-soul "
throughout ages of successive incarnations in
changing forms of ever-increasing complexity.

Darwinian evolution, a heroic effort of the
partly emancipated spirit of the age to revive
the memory of the Kabalistic formula of antiquity, " The stone becomes a plant, the plant
an animal, the animal a man, the man a spirit,
and the spirit a God," so long obscured by theological ignorance and tyranny, was only an
imperfect statement of the truth, for it ig-
nored the vital question: What is it that profits
by or needs the interminable series of transformations from the inorganic to the divine?
In this Manual a brief outline will be given
of the world-building process according to
Theosophy, but for a fuller understanding of
the subject and of the historical and scientific

corroborations of the views advanced, the student is advised to consult *The Secret Doctrine* and *Isis Unveiled,* by H. P. Blavatsky. No one has given these works a careful perusal in the spirit of honest inquiry without finding his outlook upon the past and the future profoundly modified. In connexion with the subject of this Manual the reader will find Manual No. 8, *The Doctrine of Cycles,* a help, for it treats of many cognate points which need not be repeated here. The *Century Path,* the official organ of THE UNIVERSAL BROTHERHOOD AND THEOSOPHICAL SOCIETY, has a department specially devoted to the recording and consideration of the continual stream of new scientific and archaeological discoveries which illustrate and corroborate the principles of Theosophy.

III

THREE FUNDAMENTAL PROPOSITIONS

WITHOUT going too deeply into abstract metaphysics, it is sufficient for our present purpose to know that Theosophy sees one fundamental line of progress manifesting in everything, smaller cycles repeating, in little, the process more grandly displayed in greater ones, and all being swept along in the vast cosmic periods of alternate manifestation and rest. This is the meaning of the ancient maxim repeated by the Kabalists, "As above, so below." Once understood, this law of correspondences between the action of the forces upon higher and lower planes clears up many difficulties and unveils many mysteries. It is a necessary conception in view of the existence' of Absolute Unity behind all manifestations. According to H. P. Blavatsky, the three fundamental propositions at the base of the Esoteric Philosophy are:

(a) An Omnipresent, Eternal, Boundless, and Immutable PRINCIPLE on which all speculation is impossible, since it transcends the power of human conception and could only be dwarfed by any human expression or similitude.

(b) The Eternity of the Universe *in toto* as a boundless plane; periodically "the playground of numberless Universes incessantly manifesting and disappearing," called "the manifesting stars," and the "sparks of Eternity." "The appearance and disappearance of Worlds is like a regular tidal ebb of flux and reflux."

(c) The fundamental identity of all Souls with the Universal Over-Soul, the latter being itself an aspect of the Unknown Root; and the obligatory pilgrimage for every Soul — a spark of the former — through the Cycle of Incarnation (or "Necessity") in accordance with Cyclic or Karmic law, during the whole term. In other words, no purely spiritual Buddhi (divine Soul) can have an independent (conscious) existence before the spark which issued from the pure Essence of the Universal Sixth principle, — or the OVER-SOUL — has (*a*) passed through every elemental form of the phenomenal world of that Manvantara, and (*b*) acquired individuality, first by natural impulse, and then by self-induced and self-devised efforts (checked by its Karma), thus ascending through all the degrees of intelligence, from the lowest to the highest Manas, from the mineral and plant, up to the holiest archangel (Dhyâni-Buddha). The pivotal doctrine of the Esoteric philosophy admits no privileges or special gifts in man, save those won by his own Ego through personal effort and merit throughout a long series of metempsychoses and reincarnations. — (*Secret Doctrine*, Vol. I, p. 14 *et seq.*)

The Divine Life manifests in Cycles of Eternity, vast periods of objective and subjective Being, with the object of expressing Its infinite possibilities. The Evolution of the human soul is called the " Ever-becoming," because the path of the pilgrim towards the Divine Ideal is endless, resembling the mathematical concept of an asymptote to a curve, a straight line that continually approaches yet never quite touches it, however far it may be produced. This grandiose picture of the Everbecoming, of the everlasting aspiration of the " Monad " or overshadowing Spiritual Self to an ever-widening ideal, implies its activity during past "eternities" of immense duration, alternating with periods of repose or *pralaya,* during which the results of experiences were stored up within, though they are not available to our brain-minds in their present state of imperfection. That this idea is gaining credence is seen by a perusal of popular literature; for instance Lafcadio Hearn says: " I cannot rid myself of the notion that Matter, in some blind infallible way *remembers;* and that in every unit of living substance there slumber infinite potentialities, simply because to every ultimate atom belongs the infinite and indestructible experience of billions and billions of vanished universes." . But the potentialities had to be there *first* before they could be manifested, or we should have the old absurdity of something coming out of nothing! The plan for us in this existence is to transmute and dominate the lower animal tendencies and so to obtain Self-knowledge, or unity with the Higher Self. As we do this it is possible to help the less advanced to rise more quickly, but we need not wait for full illumination before commencing humanitarian work; quite the contrary. Every uplifting thought and every unselfish deed raises the whole status of a man, even down to the " infra-atoms " composing the body which have a consciousness of their own; and every time we poison our bodies with alcohol or evil indulgence we degrade the infinitesimal lives of which our tabernacle is built. As the elect of humanity rise through inner conflict towards undreamed-of heights of compassion, wisdom, and spiritual knowledge by the attainment of the Higher Self, they will gain the power to take part in the "creative" or fashioning processes of nature. The elect of a past humanity is helping today in the " process of the suns." But for the existence of these intermediary Agencies — call them archangels, Dhyân Chohans, Gods, or what you will, who have ages ago passed through the stage in which we now are and have attained what to us would seem almost Omniscience — there would be a gap in the evolutionary scheme; a necessary hierarchy of " Builders " would be missing, and man would indeed be desolate and his future uncertain.

Science, however materialistic and short-sighted many of its votaries may be, has accepted the possibility, nay probability, of such supreme intelligences existing, through the voice of Huxley, who said that there must be beings in the universe whose intelligence is as much beyond ours as ours exceeds that of the black-beetle, and who may take an active part in the government of the natural order of things.

The divine " Creative " Principle needs intermediaries for the working out of the details of the evolutionary scheme, the main idea of which is nevertheless, *ex hypothesi*, inherent in every " atom-soul "; and although the word "gods" sounds a little strange in our ears, these supreme Agencies are as divine Beings compared with us. H. P. Blavatsky carefully pointed out that to limit the character of the Unknowable Divine Unity by *personalizing* in any way, however sublimated, would be a fundamental error, as it would make God and the Universe two separate things — two gods; but it is perfectly logical and correct to admit the existence of beings so high as to be rightfully called personal *Gods.* This the ancients knew well, but behind all the ruling divinities they believed there was a Sustainer of all: Parabrahm in India; Ain-Soph, the Hebrew secret Essence of the Kabalists; and others.

The Egyptian Hermes in the *Divine Pymander* says: "God is not a mind, but the cause that Mind is; not a spirit, but the cause that the Spirit is; not light, but the cause that the Light is."

Even in the exoteric Old Testament we find the "Gods" mentioned in many places, although efforts which cannot be called honest have been made by the translators to conceal it. In the first chapter of Genesis the word God is "Elohim," a plural term, signifying creative powers or deities; they are the same as the "Dhyânis" of Indian philosophy. In the third chapter of Genesis one of the Elohim, Jehovah, refers to the existence of others such as himself in the famous sentence: "And the Lord God (Jehovah) said: 'Behold the man is become as one of us.'"

The hierarchy of the gods, the Dhyânis, must

act strictly within the lines of the great evolutionary plan of which they are a part; their action resembles that of a breeder of pigeons, who can modify the shape and color, the size and habits of his birds within certain degrees, but cannot revolutionize their nature and turn them into hawks or owls. We ourselves even now can direct a few of the minor currents in the earth's evolution in a very small way, and we shall continue to do so in ever-increasing measure as we rise nearer to the stature of divinity, although the general plan cannot be changed. As mankind becomes conscious of the Higher Self within, overshadowing the personal self, it must develop hidden faculties capable of assimilating the mysterious and transcendental wisdom of the Gods, for the Higher Self is one with Them.

In the Current of the great Manvantaric sweep of evolution, the current of the Life-Wave, "Íśvara," composed of innumerable "Sparks" of the one Flame, descends from higher states through the material and upwards again to the spiritual, obtaining self-consciousness by the development of intellection, and enriched by the vast series of experiences gained on the pilgrimage. The stupendous Cosmic process of cyclic manifestation and withdrawal is repeated in smaller degrees, cycle within cycle, until we reach the limit of material segregation and apparent separateness — the individual personalities of men. When this is reached, progress is contingent upon the ability of the individual to throw off the veil of illusion separating one soul from another and to recognize the real unity of all. Many, many times has the " Eternal Pilgrim " to repeat this " Fall " into matter during the terrestrial journey, many times does the Higher Ego (Manas) descend from " Devachan " (a high state of spiritual existence, the " heaven which is our home" of the poets) to incarnate in the physical body through its own emanation, the brain-mind, in order to gain that experience which can be found in no other way: then to reascend to inner states of holy peace and rest again to assimilate the lessons of the last battle of life. The struggle will

continue until the sense of separateness between each man and his "other selves" (Humanity) has disappeared. H. P. Blavatsky
quotes the following from a *Catechism* of the
Eastern School in which she received instruction:

" Lift up thy head, O Lanoo; dost thou see one
or countlesss lights above thee, burning in the dark
midnight sky?"*

*" I sense one Flame, O Gurudeva, I see countless
undetached sparks shining in it."*

*" Thou sayest well. And now look around and
into thyself. That light which burns inside thee,
dost thou feel it different in anywise from the light
that shines in thy brother men?"*

*" It is in no way different, though the prisoner is
held in bondage by Karma, and though its outer
garments delude the ignorant into saying ' Thy Soul
and My Soul.' "*

The process of daily waking and sleeping,
of alternate objective lives on earth and of
subjective life in Devachan (the rest after
death), is a perfect correspondence in little
with what takes place in the history of nations,

---

* Disciple.

of races, and of worlds, culminating in the great Planetary, Solar and Universal alternations of life-activity and repose. Endless progression is the rule, and each period is higher than the last. At the close of the Rest following on the great period, or Manvantara, from out of the subjective state of Nirvâna — at present inconceivable to the majority of men because of the limitations of mind caused by passion and desire, but which is not a state of annihilation as erroneously supposed by some — the Monads will start out on a fresh pilgrimage on a higher Manvantara, possessing, in reserve, the wisdom gained in the past. This knowledge may be temporarily locked up while new experiences are being gained in other directions. This is the case with us at present, for we are only conscious of the smallest part of our mysterious past and stored-up knowledge.

In the calculations of the Orient, which in certain cases to which she gives the key H. P. Blavatsky tells us are nearly accurate, the great Mahâ-Kalpa, which includes all the lesser Manvantaras, includes one hundred " years of Brahmâ," and as each year of Brahmâ contains 360 " days and nights of Brahmâ," each 4,320,000,000 terrestrial years in length, it will be seen that the grandiose conception of Eternal progression suggested is the most impressive and awe-inspiring picture the mind can contemplate. It is a curious example of modern vanity that our age, until now bound down by the preposterous notion that the universe was only about six thousand years old, should think itself the first to spell out the letters of the word Evolution, whereas the principle has been known for ages and given out in the allegories of all nations.

Herbert Spencer made a heroic effort to put into complete form the modern theory of Evolution, and the result was a marvelously correct one considering the attitude of his school towards the world of causes, whose borderland is commonly but erroneously called the " supernatural," of which he was entirely ignorant. Spencer defines the part of the great evolutionary scheme known to him as " an integration of matter and a concomitant dissipation of motion, during which the matter passes from an indefinite incoherent homogeneity to a definite coherent heterogeneity; during which process the retained motion undergoes a parallel transformation." This definition though "coherent" is painfully limited. As he refused to recognize any kind of spiritual world, and had not even glimpsed the possibility of an astral or semi-spiritual world permeating the material world, its model and support — a half-way house to the world of causes —'his blindness to the greatest factors in the problem rendered his life-work materialistic, incomplete and ephemeral. As the materialistic school ignores the possibility of thought without the phosphated fats of the brain, it must disregard the factors of Cosmic Ideation — the Universal Mind, and the intelligent Agencies ceaselessly at work beyond the illusions of Time and Space in which we are confined. The partial version of the story of Evolution now in vogue is a stepping stone to the deeper knowledge brought by Theosophy; it looks as if mankind can only stand a little actual illumination at a time. The full blaze of Truth would be blinding.

H. P. Blavatsky says the " Esoteric Philosophy only fills the gaps made by Science and corrects her false premisses," and one of the widest gaps is the omission of the descent of spirit into matter and its ultimate ascent, the conqueror of worlds and a ruler in " heaven." It is not possible in these few pages to indicate more than the barest outline of this enormous subject, but we must carry from the outset the idea of the law of Periodicity running through all nature or confusion will result. H. P. Blavatsky took immense pains in collecting records from a large number of sources, ancient and modern, of the partial revelation of the earth's past history she was allowed to publish. Speaking of the contents of *Isis Unveiled* and *The Secret Doctrine* she says:

The proofs brought forward in corroboration of the old teaching are scattered widely throughout the old scriptures of ancient civilizations. The Purânas,

the Zendavesta and the old classics are full of them;
but no one has ever gone to the trouble of collecting and collating together those facts. The reason
for this is that all such events were recorded sym-
bolically. — (*The Secret Doctrine,* Vol. 1, p. 307)

Even in the Bible there are many corroborations of the evolutionary system of Theosophy. The first portions of Genesis when
compared with the Purânas and other antique
records, are seen to be modified and abbrevi-
ated allegorical accounts of the early history
of the universe and of mankind.

Professor Drummond in his *Lowell Lectures*
regarded Evolution as " a living power working its way through endless transformations."
Add to this the conception that the manvantaric Life sustaining all becomes subject to
limitation immediately the Divine Ideation or
Thought (the Logos or " Word ") begins to
manifest the first faint causes, the primitive
outlines of the worlds to come; and that as
matter becomes denser and form more defined
the limitations of consciousness increase. When
this is dwelt upon, the reason for the Theo-

sophical belief that there is only one heresy, the "heresy of separateness," will become clear. As long as we, as personalities, refuse to recognize *in actual life and practice* the basic Unity of that Flame whose *sparks* we are, we shall make no real progress. The principle of Universal Brotherhood without the substantial reason suggested above, would be mere sentimentality and could not stand any criticism. Once it is understood that the overshadowing Monad, or "Monads," are one spiritual unity in their essential nature, and that an isolated selfish life is an illusion of matter, every act will become a noble creative force in harmony with the "Law which moves to righteousness."

The current of the Divine Breath, "Îśvara " or Spirit (the last from *spirare,* to breathe), the out-breathing or manifestation of the activities of the One Life whose only attribute is "Eternal Motion," possesses an inherent characteristic of numerical relationship. "God geometrizes," and one of the fundamental numbers of the manvantaric period is seven. There are

seven great "divisions" of the great Breath,
which manifest in countless forms during the
Outbreathing, which is an age of such enormous duration that to us it is a veritable eternity. These seven divisions are called Tattvas,
and are manifested in the laws controlling the
physical forces of Light, Sound, the Septenary groups of the "elements" of chemistry,
etc. Science has lately proved to its satisfac-
tion that seven is the dominant number in the
sensible world, but it has not carried the discovery to its far-reaching conclusions. The
sevening principle runs through all the activities of the Cosmic process from the first faint
outbreathing at the dawn of this Manvantara
to the ordinary physiological processes of reproduction and disease in human and animal
life on the earth. There are many other numerical relationships in the descent from the
spiritual to the material, but the sevenfold
division in its simplicity and its multiples is
enough for a general comprehension of our
story of the Earth and its Rounds and Races.

IV

THE SEVEN ROUNDS

A N examination of the diagram below will
give the student some plain hints as to the
general trend of Evolution from the potential
state of existence in the One Life, Parabrahm,
(which H. P. Blavatsky speaks of as "BE-ness"
rather than Being—a subtle but very important
distinction), through the state of embodiment
in forms and then up to higher conditions.
The diagram may be applied, with the necessary modifications, to the greatest Manvantaras; the minor world-periods through which
sentient life has passed before coming into the
present one; or to the smaller cycles through
which we are passing today.   H. P. Blavatsky
gave us the clue to the labyrinth of involved
confusion as to the past history of the earth
which has come down from antiquity in legend
and symbol, so that we now can see the places

in the puzzle into which the apparently fanciful stories fit. No archaeologist has been able
to clear up and reduce to order the chaos of
fact and allusion, but now it is only necessary
to work out the details, for the design has been
laid out on the trestle board by the Custodians
of the wisdom of the ages. The following is
a brief abstract of the main plan:

From the establishment of the center of energy which is now the earth, the evolution of
life proceeds in seven clearly marked Cycles
or "Rounds," during which the Life-Wave
journeys seven times through, or better, lives
seven periods upon seven distinct "globes" or
states of existence or consciousness. The six
companion "globes" of our terrestrial sphere
are of finer substance than the earth, but it
would be a serious error to consider them as
spheres separated *in space* from the world
we live in; they should be looked upon more
as different degrees or conditions of substance,
interblending, and corresponding to different
states of consciousness. The first "globe" is
the most ethereal or shadowy (from our *pres-*

ent view-point), and the conditions surrounding the Monads starting their pilgrimage on it,
the most spiritual. Our present earth-state
is the densest and the least spiritual; the three
"globes" to come will become more ethereal
again as we progress towards perfection, and
ultimately we shall be able to leave this Earth-
Chain of " globes," as it is called for conven-
ience, to enter into still higher conditions.

The Earth-Chain of seven "globes" is the
"reincarnation" of a preceding planetary chain
on a lower evolution, of which the Moon is the
visible relic. When the Life-wave had passed
seven times round the seven "globe-conditions"
of the Lunar Chain and had assimilated all the
experience possible there, that Chain began to
die out, and instead of entering upon a period
of less activity, or "obscuration" such as all
the "globes" undergo between the Rounds, a
complete dissolution of the cohesive forces of
all the seven "globes" set in, and *after* an inter-
regnum or *pralaya,* the Lunar energies commenced to vivify a new center of " cosmic
dust " in space, and the Earth-Chain started

on its aeonian career. The Moon, scored and riven by Titanic forces, its frozen face eternally watching the earth, is the decaying shell, or corpse, of what is now the spirit or informing Principle of the Earth.

When the Life-wave on Earth shall have passed through the seven Rounds, from the most ethereal to the densest and back again to the spiritual-ethereal, the inhabitants will leave the Earth shell or corpse to decompose into Cosmic dust, but they, and its " principles," will be the richer by the vast experience gained during the wonderful pilgrimage.

We are at present about the middle point of the Fourth Round, the least spiritual Round, and we are in the Fourth "globe" too, the most material "globe" of all in each Round. We are at the time when spirit and matter are practically at an equilibrium, but we have passed the exact balancing center and so we are really on the upward grade. The process is so slow that we cannot expect to find any marked improvement in a few years, but fortunately we can hasten the speed by removing the stumbling-blocks we have planted in our own way in the past.

The only object Theosophists have in bringing this philosophy of the ages before the world, is to demonstrate the possibility and the need of greater efforts being made by mankind to raise itself. Through the spread of the true philosophy of life amongst earnest persons and the establishment of Râja Yoga Schools throughout the world, mankind will receive the seeds of the future great civilization which can only rise as a result of the actual living of brotherhood in act and thought. Theosophy thus proves that human solidarity is a fact in nature in two ways: the first by the presentation of a philosophy sound in its logic and based upon knowledge of all the facts of the case, and not merely upon material illusive appearances; secondly by actual demonstration of this philosophy of life in the lives of those who are striving against their lower natures.

CONVENTIONALIZED DIAGRAM
OF THE
LUNAR CHAIN (left) and EARTH CHAIN (right) of "Globes."

THIS diagram represents the transmission of the Life-wave from the seven "globes" of the Lunar Chain to the corresponding "globes" of the Earth Chain. Each circle represents a "globe" or state of consciousness; it must be remembered that "globes" A B C D E F G of each Chain, really interpenetrate and are interblended. They are drawn separately for clearness only. The "globes" now being considered are on the four lower planes or conditions of being, the higher three planes are formless (arûpa) and beyond the possibility of speculation for us at present.

"Globes D and D' are the physical Earth and Moon. Note that the right hand "globe" of each of the Lunar and Terrestrial pairs is a little higher up than the left hand one, showing the progress achieved. The dotted lines represent the energy passing from the Lunar conditions to the similar ones in the Earth Chain. Like all diagrams this one is very incomplete, but it may be a little help to the thoughtful student.

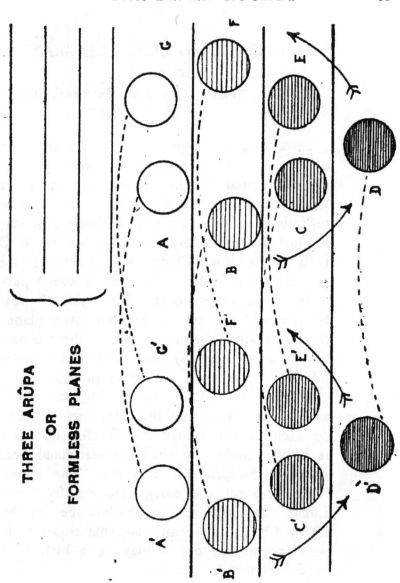

The "globes," or great planetary world-states through which the Life-wave passes in the Seven Rounds, are usually numbered from A to G, and the diagram (p. 35) will give a rough illustration of their relationship. The "globes" are not really separated by any spaces but are *fused* together; one might say that they are aspects or conditions of a single entity — Mother " Earth "; and as consciousness is different upon each, when we occupy one the rest are invisible to normal sight. " Globe " D is the present material Earth, and as it is the balancing point it is the great battle-ground where the soul has to gain the victory over the lower order of matter and material separateness — or selfishness.

H. P. Blavatsky gave an emphatic, and, as it turned out, not at all unnecessary warning of the danger of materializing ideas when they have to be reduced to diagrammatic form. The six companion "globes" of the earth through which the Life-wave takes its course must be carefully distinguished from the planets of the solar system known to astronomy;

Mars, Jupiter, etc. The globes of the Earth-chain are different gradations of consciousness, and of atomic, or perhaps interatomic, vibration, reaching from very ethereal conditions through the astral to the material, and upward again, shading into each other like the colors of the spectrum. The writer of *The Secret Doctrine* says the "globes" "are in CO-ADUNITION but not IN CONSUBSTANTIALITY WITH OUR EARTH," and thus pertain to quite different states of consciousness. The action of the hypothetical ether of space, whose vibrations are supposed to pass through the densest substances, somewhat resembles the interpenetration of one "globe" by the others.

Man (the Monad, which can only be called Man in view of later developments) passes through all the kingdoms of Nature in the First and even the Second Rounds, but it is not until the Fourth Round that the Monad — Âtmâ-Buddhi* — undergoes the awakening of the latent quality of intellection, called " the

---

* See Manual No. 2, *The Seven Principles of Man.*

descent of the Mânasaputra or Sons of Mind";
and it is not until the Third and Fourth *Root
Races* of that Fourth *Round* that what we can
recognize as present humanity appears; this
was over eighteen million years ago. In the
first Rounds the Monads have to pass "through
the . . . kingdoms in their most ethereal, filmy
and rudimentary forms in order to clothe
themselves in and assimilate the nature of the
newly formed chain." This primitive condition is far more ethereal than any form of
matter with which chemistry is acquainted;
compared with it the most nebulous fire-mist
would be coarser than granite is denser than
hydrogen gas; it is almost subjective, almost
unmanifested. The development of humanity
as we know it is the subject of Manual 18, in
which the process of life through the Races
on "globe" D, in the present Round, the
Fourth, will be considered.

As the subject of this sketch is quite new
to many readers it will be well, before going
farther, to summarize its main features.

I. The spirit in man (called the " Monad "

or Âtmâ-Buddhi) is immortal both in the
past and in the future. It has lived many
lives on earth, the intervals between which
have been spent in rest and assimilation of
what it has learned.

2. The great process of the evolution of the
Universe consists in the gradual descent of
spiritual conditions into material ones and then
the return to the primal state *plus* the experience gained. This evolution applies to the
past of man as well as to that of Nature in
general, for the law of cyclic progression is
endless.

3. The process of the special evolution in
which we are at present immersed carries us
through seven great journeys or " Rounds "
during which the Monad or Ray of the Divine,
which is our Higher SELF, gains experience in
seven conditions of substantial existence,
called " Globes." These seven "globe-conditions" are passed through seven times during
the terrestrial evolution, each journey being
one Round, a period of enormous duration.
On each of the Rounds the Monad finds the

conditions denser than the last until it reaches the Fourth. Then more ethereal conditions begin to reappear, and the Fifth and Sixth Rounds become increasingly immaterial, until the last Round will find man a godlike being living in harmony with the most spiritual conditions in Nature.

4. We are just past the middle of the Spiral of spirals, the balancing point of spirit and matter, and the great struggle for each unit now is to throw himself consciously into harmony with the advancing spiritual wave. Those who fail to work in unison with the divine plan will be rejected from the Master's House, though not until after every possible opportunity has been given them to reform, and they will have to recommence the long journey at some future date. It is possible to resist the march of progress for a while, and to act as a brake on the wheel, but not for ever.

5. In each "globe" there are many races or types through which the Monad gains almost infinite experiences. On the Earth, the densest

of all the "globes," there are seven great human Root-Races, one succeeding another (our Black, Yellow, Red and White Races are minor subdivisions, not the Root-Races of which we are speaking). We are in the Fifth Root-Race and are therefore beyond the densest point of materiality and are on the slow upward climb. There are seven sub-races in each Root-Race, and innumerable family races and blends. We are in the fifth sub-race of the Fifth Root-Race.

6. The process of human evolution during the first Rounds and well on into the Fourth consists in the formation of a conscious vehicle, the lower animal-man (not the Darwinian "missing link"), which becomes overshadowed by the Intelligence, the " Manas " or Mind-Principle, which has itself pursued its own course of evolution. This blending of the Mind or Manas with the non-intelligent — from our poor human mental standpoint — but intensely spiritual Monad, which is the energizing force behind the mindless embryonic animal-man, is the making of man as a *con-*

sciously responsible being. This takes place during the Third Root-Race on this terrestrial globe, at a period of about eighteen million years ago. Since then there have been many rises and falls and many alternations of barbarism and civilization; continents have risen out of the waters and others have been destroyed by flood and fire, and man has gained his dearly-bought experience; but the Higher Ego has not yet had time to gain the upper hand, except in the rarest cases.

7. In each Round certain different principles of our compound nature are evolved from potentiality into action and certain Elements in outer nature are developed in harmony with them; the next step will be the manifestation of matter in more refined or ethereal forms and of more potent forces than those we know today; but this period is still far distant.

The remembrance of our marvelous past is locked up in the mysterious chambers of the Higher Ego; the brain-mind, which was only e-volved "yesterday," cannot penetrate into these sacred arcana until it has arrived at the pure condition of impersonality which will permit the Higher to unite fully with it. Even in certain abnormal states, cataleptic and other, extraordinary powers of memory can be displayed. These are the functions of the astral man, and although surprising, are nothing to the semi-omniscience of the Higher nature.

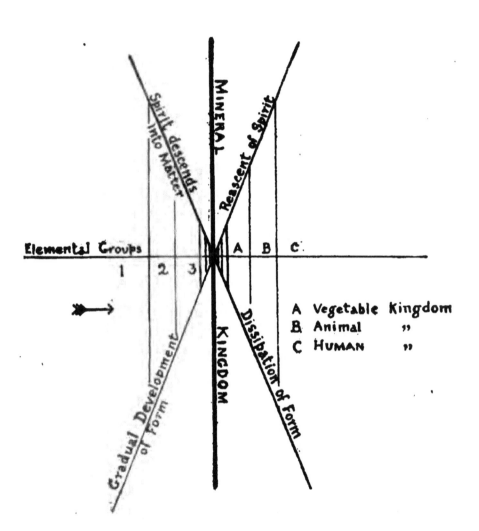

Elemental Groups

1 2 3

Spirit descends into Matter

MINERAL

Reascent of Spirit

A B C

KINGDOM

Dissipation of Form

Gradual Development of Form

A Vegetable Kingdom
B Animal   "
C Human   "

V

THE SEVEN KINGDOMS

IN the stupendous effort of the One Life —
the "Unconscious" of some German philosophers — to express Itself in ever-advancing
degrees during the evolution and destruction
of universes, the descent of spirit into matter
is carried on, according to the law of correspondences, by means of Planetary Chains. Of
course these chains may be of infinite variety,
and of those connected with the other planets
of the Solar System we have not yet been given
definite information. We shall therefore necessarily confine our study to the Earth-chain.
Although all the other planets, except Neptune,
are closely connected with us in many ways,
they are themselves planetary chains upon
which distinct waves of life are flowing. We
should not feel at home upon any other planetary chain, because we have not had the age-

long preparation for the entirely different conditions prevailing elsewhere. But although the other planets are not in *our* chain, many of them exert a powerful influence on earth-life, though Science has not yet traced their action. The Moon especially exerts such an influence, although it is " dead." Being the " Mother " of the Earth, its influence is peculiar. Physics can see no more in the Moon than its attractive action in lifting the tides on the Earth, but Theosophy traces results of the former existence of terrestrial life on the Lunar Chain in many other directions, which will be considered later. Then again Occult Science calls the Earth the "adopted child and younger brother" of Venus in one aspect, and its " Twin Sister " in another aspect — size, speed of rotation, etc. *Venus is far in advance of us* in development, and it is a singular "coincidence" that that planet has been seen on a few occasions to be self-luminous or phosphorescent. The writer of these pages once had the good fortune to see this remarkable phenomenon, of which astronomy gives no explanation. Possibly the inhabitants have discovered the secret of the glow-worm and are self-luminous!! Mercury is also ahead of us in its life history, but Mars is a little behind, and is at present under a minor "obscuration" or suspension of its highest activities.

The statement in *The Secret Doctrine* that Neptune is connected very slightly with the sun receives some confirmation from recent discoveries showing that its atmospheric spectrum shows unique features; and its extreme distance suggests the need of a different evolutionary scheme from that of the rest of the planets. It is the only one of the planets that disobeys Bode's rhythmic Law of distances.

As the Monad travels in its spiral progress around the seven " globes," it first becomes imprisoned in three successive kingdoms of " Elementals " or Nature-Forces; then in the Mineral, Vegetable and Animal kingdoms, finally gaining self-consciousness as Man, for there are really *seven* sentient kingdoms in Nature, and no " dead matter " at all, though science

has not yet learned anything about the three
Elemental kingdoms, and has hardly dared to
recognize the obscure consciousness in the Mineral, of which chemical affinity is one manifestation. The kingdoms of the Elemental
semi-intelligent forces are very difficult to understand, and little definite information has
been given to us about them; but we can glean
from the few teachings available that in passing through those stages the Monad is experiencing the peculiar consciousness of the "automatic" and semi-"automatic" natural forces
which have a different consciousness from that
of even the lowest animal. A reference to the
diagram on page 44 will make it clear that
the Monad was in a lower condition when in
the Elemental kingdoms than even when locked
up in the Mineral, through which the Life-
wave has to pass before rising to the Vegetable
and onward up through the Animal forms to
the union with (*or awakening to the descent
of*) the Mânasic principle, which has been pur-
suing another line of evolution, and which is
what makes us Man (from a Sanskrit root

" MAN " to *think*), the highly complex being now embodied in the tenement of clay.

The Monad must not be regarded as having obtained separate individuality in the lower kingdoms during the time the vestures were being organized and prepared for the incarnation of the *human intelligences* (*Mânasaputra* = Sons of Mind) to come. The first faint beginnings of the spiritual flame dividing into units is suggested in the vegetable kingdom, or even in the mineral as in the families or groups of "elements," but there it is hardly more than a dim potentiality. In the highest animals the sense of individuality is almost attained; but it is the prerogative of the Monad only after the descent of the Mânasic element, making it Man — a " Thinker " — to possess and fully comprehend the sense of *self*-consciousness, of apparent *self*-identity or *personality*. This illusory feeling of separateness must be gained: it is a part of the training resulting from the immersion of the lower Manas — the shadow of the Higher — in Matter; but it must be struggled with and van-

quished and seen for what it really is, before
the Unity of all beings can be understood.
It is by this struggle that progress is made
in spiritual life. Spiritual life is the actual
realization of the Unity of all, and Compassion, Peace and Wisdom are its natural concomitants.

VI

THE "COATS OF SKINS"

THERE is a wide abyss between the Theosophical teaching upon the important subject of the Evolution of Humanity and the hypothesis of biology in vogue today, with its materialistic affirmation of the descent of intellectual and spiritual man from nothing but a supposed race of brutes, ancestors of the anthropoid apes and of ourselves. This popular ape-ancestry idea recognizes man as nothing but a more highly specialized animal with a larger cranial capacity produced by the blind struggle for existence and other physical causes. Science has nothing to tell us of a spiritual principle existing before birth and surviving the death of the body. It knows nóthing of the evolution of the Mânasic or Human Soul. It repudiates a " tendency towards progress " in any special direction, at-

tributing the existing complexities to " accidental favorable variations or 'sports' " acting
in harmony with the conditions of environment.
The materialistic hypothesis of Evolution ignores any pushing force or Intelligence behind
the visible phenomena, and reduces its adherents to the curious dilemma of explaining the
building up of the complex nature of man with
his marvelous intellect and feelings, the moral
and spiritual attributes of conscience, judgment, reason, etc., by laws of chance! The
laws of mere physical action and reaction to
varying stimuli which are supposed to have
brought about the present state of things
could as easily work downwards to the destruction of highly organized intelligences;
Huxley says the possibility of the Thames valley becoming unfit for human life and only
being able to support that of the jungle or
the desert is quite reasonable and would be
an example of the survival of the fittest. If
we imagine a complete change in terrestrial
conditions through some " accidental " cause,
such as a sudden increase of the sun's energy,

man would soon disappear, a "discreditable episode upon one of the meanest of the planets." The abyss between Theosophy and materialistic science is further shown in the doleful prospect the latter holds out that when living beings die out for want of water or heat there will be nothing left as the outcome of all the past activity but a horrid blank! and as the alternative, the orthodox creeds offer the illogical and puerile notion that one life spent on earth by a just-"created" soul, is sufficient to decide its whole future fate, and that it passes into some "supernatural" state of which we can know nothing while here.

But to return to the materialistic hypothesis, which demands acceptance from the thinking world under pain of intellectual contempt and ostracism, we find that notwithstanding its claim to uphold the existence of the unerring Law of Cause and Effect, it really accepts the idea of Fortuity, of chance, and of secondary causes producing primary effects. Theosophy teaches that if anything *evolves*, it must have had the potentiality of its future *in*volved within itself which had to come out sooner or later, and it asserts that science simply needs to get rid of prejudice and to set about its investigations in a new way — in a *natural* way — to find that intelligent law does reign in nature and that there does exist a tendency towards progress pushing consciousness into higher and higher degrees. Theosophy, of course, admits the operation of the laws of Selection and of the Survival of the Fittest, *within certain limits,* as *secondary* laws *only,* but it shows plainly that these are but *secondary* causes, modifying agents of the great irresistible flow of the Monadic stream of evolution. Theosophy, with its wide outlook over past time, shows that the world *cannot* lose the power of supporting intelligent manifested life until the cycle closes and the stream of Monads overflows into the preparation for the rebirth in a higher Chain. Patanjali, the great Indian philosopher and teacher of the Yoga Philosophy, said ages ago that Nature energizes for the soul's experience; and according to the ancient Wisdom — Theosophy

— the attainment of full self-consciousness of
its greatness and of its divine powers by the
god within, is the present aim of evolution.
Once this is attained a glorious Path opens
out, transcending all imagination. H. P. Blavatsky says in *The Secret Doctrine:*

Between man and the animal — whose Monads (or
Jīvas) are fundamentally identical — there is the impassable abyss of Mentality and Self-consciousness.
What is human mind in its higher aspect, whence
comes it, if it is not a portion of the essence —
and, in some rare cases of incarnation, the *very
essence* — of a higher Being: one from a higher
and divine plane? Can man — a god in the animal
form — be the product of Material Nature by evolution alone, even as is the animal, which differs from
man in external shape, but by no means in the
materials of its physical fabric, and is informed by
the same, though undeveloped, Monad — seeing that
the intellectual potentialities of the two differ as the
Sun does from the Glow-worm? And what is it
that creates such difference, unless man is an animal
plus a *living god* within his physical shell?

Turning to the diagram on page 35, and
keeping in mind the warning against material-

izing such things too rigidly, notice that the
dotted lines passing from each lunar " globe "
to a corresponding but higher earth " globe,"
may represent the awakening of life on earth
by the arrival of the Monad — or perhaps we
may now say, with due reserve, the Monads,
in their seven stages of progress. The lunar
" ancestors," the ethereal vestures of the Monads, called Pitris or Fathers, commence to project their "doubles" onto earth but are not at
first individualized under the new conditions
of the primitive ethereal or almost immaterial
"globes" of the early Rounds; still on the first
terrestrial "globe" (A.), that portion of the
Monadic essence which has gained the greatest possible experience upon the Lunar Chain
starts upon its new pilgrimage with more
energy than the other six divisions, and rapidly pushes ahead, working out forms of shadowy substance into more and more suitable
vehicles for the reception of the Human Intellect, the link between the Monad and the
lower vestures. The three together compose
the complete Man (the seven principles are

subdivisions of these three). This class reaches segregated individuality very slowly in actual measurement of time, but quickly when compared with the other "laggards." The remaining six divisions gradually incarnate on the Earth-Chain until all have arrived. A few of the most advanced reach the "human germ-stage" in the First Round, and make such progress that their astral vestures soon begin to acquire a certain individuality, in the Second and Third Rounds, though they are still very ethereal and are not yet possessed of mind. But those Monads occupying animal forms (physical) after the middle of the Fourth Round will not become men at all in *this* Chain, with the exception of some of the anthropoid apes. This subject is treated further in Manual 18.

The vestures of the soul, the semi-conscious astral forms to the plan of which the physical body gradually conformed, and the passional Desire-principle, "Kâma," were formed by projection from the Lunar Chain first; and afterwards when the hour struck, the Higher

Manas (or Higher "Ego") settled in and illuminated the semi-conscious forms. Even yet we are hardly conscious of the higher condition of existence of the Ego; and of the sustaining and illuminating Monad — Âtmâ-Buddhi — the ordinary man has practically no knowledge at all. It may seem strange to speak of a portion of the human soul so far removed from daily life that the *personal* self may pass a lifetime without recognizing its existence, but the fact is that we know little or nothing of the profounder depths of our nature: that glorious heritage of wisdom is the ultimate reward of victory over personal selfishness. But psychologists are aware, though they have not followed their observations to their logical conclusion, that the lower mind may act for half a lifetime in a partly idiotic condition, while the judgment and higher qualities are in abeyance, and suddenly the intellect may resume its sway as if nothing had happened. Du Prel gives a curious illustration of the presence of the clear intelligence in a state of suspended animation for years, but not decayed nor feeble in the least. He quotes from Dr. Wolfart's researches on Mesmerism the case of a patient who had been idiotic for thirteen years and yet manifested perfect intelligence, memory, and normal sanity, upon falling into the somnambulistic condition, in which she even referred to the fear she had expressed before her misfortune, lest her brain-power should fail. It was only when in the somnambulistic state that she could communicate her rational thoughts. This occurred only a few times and she died apparently insane. This and other similar cases shows that high intelligence may be latent, and only waiting for its opportunity to manifest. So it is with the Higher Ego; it so seldom gets the opportunity of unveiling that most persons are unaware of its existence. When it succeeds in showing a fraction of its Light we say — Lo, a genius!

The substance of the "globes" in the early Rounds, and of the first "globes" in this Round, is not of the nature of present molecular matter. Its subtlety is entirely different from that of hydrogen or helium, those lightest of gases. H. P. Blavatsky says it may fitly be called " astral," meaning " starry, shining or pellucid, in various and numerous degrees from a quite filmy to a viscid state," and although in later periods it arrived ("material-ized ") nearer to the condition of the thinnest gases we know, there will be endless confusion if it is not plainly understood that the matter of the primitive degree would not be percep-tible to our physical senses or instruments, which are adapted to slower and much less intense vibrations. The Monadic essence, in passing through the preparatory pilgrimage necessary before the beginning of intellectual life was possible, clothes itself in the most filmy and ethereal suggestions of the future mineral, vegetable, and animal kingdoms in order to assimilate the nature of the newly formed Chain. As the different "globe-states" are experienced by the pilgrim on its journey, a gradual densifying takes place in its own constitution and in its environment in each Round until the Fourth, during which Round the reascent into the spiritual condition commences. The Fourth Round being the densest, and "globe" D in each Round being at the bottom of the spiral, we find ourselves in the position when spirit and matter are nearly in equilibrium, for we are on "globe" D in the Fourth Round *now*. We are, however, beyond the pivotal point of matter and spirit. Each "globe" of the seven forming our chain supports seven great Root Races of mankind in succession, and we are now past the Fourth Root Race and well on in the Fifth, and so are on the upward climb though not out of danger yet.

H. P. Blavatsky says that

every "Round," (on the descending scale) is but a repetition in a more concrete form of the Round that preceded it, as every globe — down to our fourth sphere (the actual earth) — is a grosser and more material copy of the more shadowy sphere which precedes it in their successive order, on the three higher planes. . . . Every Round, as well as every subsequent globe . . . having been, and still having to be the arena of the same evolution, only repeated each time on a more solid material basis.—(*The Secret Doctrine,* vol. II, 256, *et passim*)

In studying the diagram on page 35, notice that the seven "globes" are on the four lower planes of being, and that each right hand "globe" is a little higher than the corresponding left hand one. This shows the progressive flow of the life-wave. It is noteworthy that "globe" D, the present earth, is alone on its plane and stands as if it contained the potentialities of all the rest, which are displayed above.

Science has no record of the life that existed in the primitive nebula out of which the physical earth consolidated, for nothing which our physical eyes could read has been imprinted upon the whirling mass of attenuated vapor. There were no stratified rocks to preserve the impressions of the rudimentary centers of life, even if they had any forms, but Theosophy affirms that some kind of organized life has never been absent from our earth since the first ethereal state of the Fire-mist, long antecedent to what physical science believes the earliest date, for it shows that "no evolution is possible without the Monad as the vivifying agent" (W. Q. Judge). There is no dead matter, the earth is a living thing, the body, as the ancients believed, of a great goddess, and its progress cannot be separated from that of humanity. The student will find valuable clues to the spiritual nature and consciousness of the atom in *The Secret Doctrine*.

The idea of ethereal states preceding the material is so novel to most people of Western training and is so important for the understanding of the true scheme of Evolution, that it is necessary to give a little more attention to it. The idea of a semi-material body being built up around the Monad on a semi-material earth is not unreasonable when materialistic prejudice is laid aside, and the existence of one such body within the physical frame at the present day has been amply proved by the researches of a few bold men of science who have dared to defy the sneers of their ill-informed colleagues. Among others Sir W. Crookes, Dr. A. R. Wallace, M. Camille Flammarion, and more recently Professor Botazzi of the Naples University, have been successful in demonstrating the existence of the "astral double." That this ethereal counterpart of the physical body, invisible to normal sight usually, enwrapped fiber to fiber with the flesh, ("clothed in skins" according to the allegory of the Rounds and Races in Genesis) can exude from the body and display under certain rare conditions a partly independent existence and a surprising coherence and energy, is now established by the rigorous experiments of the acute observers who have satisfactorily eliminated the hypothesis of fraud. Of course this astral double or "eidolon" is not the soul; it has no mind or conscience of its own; and there is nothing really new in this supposed discovery. It was universally known in antiquity and is widely credited today by multitudes who have not had their intelligences warped by materialism. The Egyptians had an accurate scientific knowledge of its functions and painted or carved the *Ka* or double at the side of the living man on the walls of the tombs and temples. The existence of this ethereal vesture of the soul being proved, the question naturally arises: How did it originate? The answer, which requires a fuller treatment of the action of the Lunar Pitris, is discussed in Manual 18, but a remark of H. P. Blavatsky, written at the time when the grossest misrepresentation and crucifixion was the reward of that brave pioneer, is worth careful thought by those who look for corroborations of the Esoteric Philosophy:

The whole issue between the profane and the esoteric sciences depends upon the belief in, and demonstration of, the existence of an astral body within the physical, the former independent of the latter. — (*The Secret Doctrine*)

MATTER AND FORCE

THE Nebular Theory of Laplace has been found wanting of late, and many other attempts to solve the mystery of the earth's formation have been made with little more success than the demonstration of the high probability that there was a primitive nebula out of which the physical world condensed. We see many forms of nebulae, but the spiral form with two centers has recently been discovered to be the commonest type, an important corroboration of a fundamental principle in Occult Science, *i. e.*, the duality of all forces. Some of the shapes of the nebulae seem inexplicable upon the ordinary hypothesis of condensation, but there is no reason to suppose that they are all in the same phase of existence. However this may be, and no doubt astronomy will bring many new factors to light

which will clear up much that is obscure in
the physical development of nebulae, Theosophy carries back the origin of the Earth-Chain
far beyond the manifestation of the nebulous
matter visible to our senses, into astral conditions not subject to physical tests, though
they have left, nevertheless, their imperishable
records, which can be read by those who have
the right to investigate.

The various nebular hypotheses are helps to
some understanding of the " descent of spirit
into matter," though they only take into consideration the condensation of ordinary matter.
Physical science has no means, as yet, of -
tracing the origin of the matter of which the
nebulae are composed, but some daring speculations have lately been made by advanced
thinkers which show an approach to Theosophy.

For instance, Professor S. Newcomb, the
well-known American astronomer, and a conservative thinker, ventures to criticize the
hitherto-accepted belief in the eternity of matter. He says:

But we doubt whether any physical philosopher of the present day would be satisfied to accept any determination of the eternity of matter. All he would admit is that as far as his observation goes, no change in the quantity of matter can be produced by any known cause. . . . But he would at the same time admit that his experience no more sufficed to settle the question than the observation of an animal for a single day would settle the duration of its life, or prove that it had neither a beginning nor an end. He would probably admit that even matter itself may be the product of evolution.

This is a striking admission from a scientific authority; the last sentence is pure occultism.

From the wider evolutionary standpoint of Eastern philosophy, which includes the spiritual aspect of the universe as well as the material in its scope, the necessity of matter having evolved from an invisible condition is apparent. Theosophy carries the imagination back to a state in which the Solar System was trembling on the verge of Becoming, and to the time when a new condensation was preparing for the development of the worlds as theaters of life and evolution. This condition, of course,

precedes the ethereal. The observations of
Zöllner, an unfortunate German scientist who
was in advance of his time, Sir W. Crookes,
and others, have brought out undeniable proofs
of the possibility of at least the temporary
materialization of invisible substance. Zöllner
recorded a curious apparition he observed of
a jet of water spouting in every direction
from a point in the air, as if from an explos-
ive center. This is exactly what should happen
if astral invisible matter from another plane
of existence had been suddenly materialized,
condensed, so to speak, and poured into the
physical plane through an invisible " leak."
Lovers of humanity who wish to penetrate
deeply into nature's laws to use their knowledge unselfishly, must know that by the
study of the laws governing the intelligent
and semi-intelligent forces behind the familiar
forms of matter, an infinitely valuable knowledge of *causes* may be gained, causes of which
the phenomenal effects we now see are but the
inevitable concomitants. But like Sigurd, who
understood the voices of the birds in the forest

after tasting the dragon's blood, this hidden world cannot be entered until the dragon of selfishness and personality has been slain within us, the dragon that keeps humanity from the golden fruit of the Tree of Knowledge *and* Life. Modern science in its experimental research does not recognize that the knowledge of nature's processes in the ultimates — the only real Wisdom — is not — *cannot* be — separated from altruism and the highest morality. The key to attainment is in the aspirant himself; the desire to obtain knowledge solely to place it on the altar of humanity. is the only one that leads to Enlightenment. Everything else is illusionary or evanescent.

There are certain fundamental divisions or aspects of the universal Cosmic Life, the seven "Tattvas," spiritual and invisible at one pole, but appearing at the other in the form of the physical forces of Light, Heat, Electricity or Gravitational attraction and Repulsion (the latter not yet recognized by physical science), etc. Control of the passions and desires, efforts to lead a really altruistic life and to sink the lower personal egotism, gradually lead to the acquirement of a state of impersonal wisdom in which the Adept becomes conscious of his unity with the higher intellectual and spiritual aspects of these forces, the higher pole. The attainment of this wisdom is not the outcome of any ordinary process of mental application alone, such as a University course, but is the culmination of many lives of endeavor to break down the wall separating the " me " and " thee." The arcane knowledge is the opening of the inner perception. Nothing but absolute selflessness will bring the world to the point where it can begin the study of the real causes of the phenomena of nature; causes never to be understood by the ordinary personal man, however brilliantly endowed with intelligence. The greatest thinkers today are reasoning entirely upon the basis supplied by the physical senses, but there are a few highly developed souls who have broken through the veil of time and space. These stand as Protectors and Guardian Walls for humanity, unknown philosophers of altruism; but in time, all men will open their hearts to the higher truths. Theosophy evokes a picture of the future so glorious that the mind hardly dares believe it, yet it is no fanciful vision, laboriously built up from ingenious guesses of what might be, but is the result of actual knowledge of the nature and powers of the Higher Self by those Teachers who sent H. P. Blavatsky with a few crumbs to feed the hungry. The Elect of the present humanity will be the guides and instructors of a future mankind whose Monads are now imprisoned, semi-conscious, in the most intelligent of the animal kingdom, or perhaps are struggling in the lower ranks. The hierarchies of spiritual " Builders " at present controlling the ethereal machinery of the universe are the Elect of past humanities; and it is even hinted that to be an "atom" in some future Manvantara will be higher than to be a human being now!

Returning a moment to the Tattvas and the atoms of science. We have no clear idea what an atom is — an electron still less, as, according to the postulate it cannot have parts or size nor can it rotate or turn upside down. Theosophy cuts the Gordian knot and declares from knowledge that the atoms are centers of consciousness — *lives,* and therefore *Metaphysical, i. e.,* beyond the physical that we measure and weigh. The Tattvas play through them; in fact, they are the Tattvas in one form. The Tattvas, in their higher aspects, are the higher principles in us; as we gain self-control, we gain control of the whole range of the Tattvas. The Adept uses them consciously. H. P. Blavatsky was severely criticised for refusing to believe in the existence of inorganic matter and for endowing atoms with intelligence, yet we find many of the brightest minds of today accepting the same; for instance, Edison says:

I do not believe matter is inert, acted upon by an outside force. To me it seems that every atom is possessed by a certain amount of primitive intelligence: look at the thousand ways in which atoms of hydrogen combine with those of other elements. . . . Do you mean to say they do this without intelligence?

A great Theosophical Teacher says nature is ever attempting to attain consciousness in organic rather than inorganic forms. Many illustrations of the action of the divine Creative Wisdom, the Intelligence behind all the Forces — Eros, the oldest of the Gods according to Plato — the divine Ray or " Fohat," in the production of the Earth-Chain, are given in *The Secret Doctrine,* but one important form of its action must again be referred to here, *i. e.,* that the law of progress in time and space, physically and metaphysically, is spiral. This spiral process is polarized after leaving the One Unity, so we find Fohat manifesting in duality throughout all nature. This is the root of the " pairs of opposites," the " Love and Hate " of Empedocles, the positive and negative. The energizing Fire, Fohat, is said to hiss as it glides hither and thither in serpentine coils; this is the root idea of the Serpent allusions found in all symbology, and it played a prominent part in all the allegories of the Mysteries. Christianity is not exempt from it, for Jesus said: " Be ye wise as

serpents," etc. As the spot of undifferentiated
" cosmic dust," or " laya center," in which the
new earth started was "informed by the freed
principles of a just deceased sidereal body,"
it became serpentine, something of the nature
of a comet, and then collecting more and more
ethereal " dust " condensed into a brilliant sun-
like body, which gradually settled down into
a state habitable by material forms.

According to the archaic teachings we should
expect to find evidence in the starry spaces of
the dual action of Fohat; and such evidence
is forthcoming, for the results of the photo-
graphic charting of the heavens have shown an
enormous number of nebulae — the majority
— to be spiral, and to stream from two centers
in twining wreaths of luminous haze. The
ancient Greeks considered the " law of verti-
cal movement in primordial matter " to be
fundamental, and the very latest speculation
of modern physics is that each atom is composed of immense numbers of "corpuscles"
of " negative electricity " moving in rapid
rotation. We are just re-discovering what

has been lost in the night of the dark ages.

Fohat also energizes another kind of spiral, a cyclic spiral, for the paths of the celestial bodies are spiral curves of the utmost complexity. No astronomer has plotted out the *real* path of the Moon, for instance, which is composed of (1) its own motion round the earth, (2) the earth's orbit round the sun, and (3) the solar motion in its mysterious course. The action of Fohat in primeval space is thus given in *The Secret Doctrine:*

Fohat turns with his two hands, in contrary directions, the "seed" and the "curds" or Cosmic Matter; in clearer language is turning particles in a highly attenuated condition, and nebulae.—(Vol. I, p. 672)

The descent of the Monad into Matter and its pilgrimage through the seven Rounds on the seven "globes," is the effect of the spiral working of Fohat in time, and here again the dual action is well marked. The Monad is the substratum of the *dual* intellectual and psycho-physical evolutions which ultimately unite in forming the perfect man, each process having been spiral in itself.

VIII

CORRESPONDENCES IN EVOLUTION

H. P. BLAVATSKY warned her pupils
that the teachings and interpretations
of the hidden symbolism of antiquity which she
was giving were only a very small portion of
the whole philosophy in the possession of the
Masters of Wisdom; and that according to the
reception given by the world to the hints given,
so would be the future opportunities of obtaining more light. We have to bear in mind then,
that to understand the ideal framework of the
universe, necessary faculties will have to be
developed in us which are yet in embryo. We
must never forget that behind the general outline of the Rounds and "globes" there must be
much more hidden meaning. Certain expon-
ents of Theosophy in the earlier days of the
Society, whose considerable lucidity of expression rendered them qualified to place the broad

facts before the reading public, showed a tendency to materialize them in harmony with the materialistic trend of thought at that time; but H. P. Blavatsky was most emphatic in urging that not until we come to the consideration of the human race on *"globe" D, in our Fourth Round,* do the conditions become fairly comprehensible to our present brain-intellection, for the early Rounds and the states of consciousness which the Monad passed through in them are matters about which we may only speculate with the greatest caution.

While we know that we shall not have to unlearn anything that has been definitely established by H. P. Blavatsky, she herself pointed out that some of her teachings were in forms suitable for beginners — for in these tremendous subjects the most acute minds are only spelling out the A, B, C — and that the partial expression and elucidation of the mysteries of nature and being which we have received will not find its full exposition until the world develops the faculties for comprehending it.

Having been thus warned that there is more

meaning in every record than appears at first sight, we may try to get some idea, even if an incomplete one, of the passing over of the life-forms from the Lunar to the Terrestrial Chain.

The spiritual units called the Monad or Monads (it is difficult to draw a dividing line between what is really One Light, though multiple in Rays) whose evolution upon the Earth-Chain is being studied, come in a stream of which various parts are in different stages of progress, for they are not newly created " out of nothing." As they leave the last Round of the Lunar-Chain to start on their journey into matter on the higher Earth-Chain, the most advanced portions of the stream may be called the " potentially human." These are destined to pass before the others through the first Rounds and "globes," reaching the really human condition before the least developed Monads have reached the dense mineral embodiment. Then in order of progress and activity come the " potential " animal, vegetable, mineral, higher elemental, middle elemental and lower elemental, the one class *shading into the other.* As the matter of the first Rounds and "globes" was very unsubstantial in comparison with the present physical, the forms of life were equally so — mere shadowy sketches, so to speak, of future possibilities. They were the archetypes or thought-forms of the coming complete worlds. It is impossible for us to grasp more than a vague picture of the conditions prevailing at this period, and to express anything about it in words is full of the danger of misconception. As space is so limited, it is impossible to dwell at length on the subject or to give illustrations which make it clearer; for the most complete account of these difficult points the Stanzas of the Book of Dzyan and the Commentaries given in *The Secret Doctrine* must be consulted. Their poetical language and the illuminating expositions of H. P. Blavatsky convey positive impressions to intuitive minds. What is not transmitted may be safely left until we unveil the faculties necessary for the comprehension of these spiritual and ethereal states. There can be no rigid lines drawn in Theosophical teachings : Katherine Tingley and all the Teachers of Theosophy have told us that the time will come when all sincere workers for humanity will obtain absolute certainty concerning these and other mysteries; but it will not be by ordinary methods of instruction such as a typical University course, but chiefly through healthy and normal development of the powers of the Higher Ego, the real Man, enabling them to investigate and prove for themselves. Theosophy does not encourage the so-called dogmatic style of teaching. Those who know the facts beyond all possibility of doubt are the least dogmatic; they say, " The facts are thus and thus, and if you investigate the right way, with a pure motive and a ready mind, you can prove them for yourself." It is a source of great pleasure to the pupils of H. P. Blavatsky to find so many of her teachings which were scouted by the wiseacres of her time, now being accepted as established facts; but the proofs of the deeper mysteries she referred to, and many other parts of the philosophy that she held in reserve, cannot be approached by the means at the disposal of physical science, which does not recognize the necessity of purity of life as an essential factor before the unveiled truth can be approached.

One feature in the general plan of development is of primary importance as it is reflected in many minor degrees, *i. e.,* that each successive Round is more material than the last, until the Fourth Round is reached, and also that the lower "globes" in every Round are denser than the higher ones. "Globe" D contains all the potentialities of the rest and co-exists with them until the close of the life-period on the Chain, once it has become consolidated. Our visible moon, "globe" D of the Lunar Chain, the most material, has not yet decomposed, though it is in process of constant dissolution.

It is well known to Physiology, and still more completely worked out in Theosophy, that the human embryo runs through the past stages of human life in its ante-natal development, and as it passes through the stages the race has experienced (far more complex than anthropology knows yet) in a few months, so the potential human Monad passes through the Second and Third Rounds at a rapid pace in comparison with the slow progress of the laggards — the less progressed Monads. In the Second Round there is a change in the order of development for a while, but we need not discuss that here as it does not materially affect the plan. In each Round a new " Element " is manifested, and as we pass through the three future Rounds we shall become familiar with states of Matter at present utterly unknown, but which are lying latent (for us) and waiting until we develop the senses to appreciate them. Each cycle or Round specially develops one human principle, and as we are now in the Fourth Round, we find the principles up to the fourth, the Kâmic, the passional-emotional one, in full sway; but, as we have passed the fourth Root *Race* of this Round and are now in the fifth Root Race, the intellectual principle has gained strength, though it is necessarily governed by the passional undertone, or tonic, of the whole Round.

The key-note of the next or Fifth Round will be the higher Intellectual or Mânasic principle; that of the Sixth Round, Buddhi, the Spiritual Soul; and the Seventh Round will shine forth in the full radiance of Âtmâ, which includes all. Those who have slain the tiger of self, have carried themselves over the critical stage of the battle mankind is now waging, into the Fifth or even Sixth Round conditions, and are "the saved," forerunners of what the entire Race will be ages hence.

The great cycle of the Rounds and Races is repeated in the life-cycle of the individual man. His astral body is built up as a matrix for the physical, which is formed on its model; then passion and sex develop later in life, intellect becomes dominant, and towards the close of his earthly career should come a higher spiritual perception. Not only is the cycle repeated in human life, but in intra-uterine development the embryo traces the same course: sex becomes distinguishable in the third month, the convolutions of the brain associated with thought appear at the fifth, and the seven-months old child is capable of independent existence. *The Secret Doctrine* says:

On strict analogy, the cycle of Seven Rounds in their work of the gradual formation of man through every kingdom of Nature, are repeated on a microscopical scale in the first seven months of gestation of a future human being. Let the student think over and work out this analogy. As the seven-months-old unborn baby, though quite ready, yet needs two months more in which to acquire strength and consolidate; so man, having perfected his evolution during seven Rounds, remains two periods more in the womb of mother-Nature before he is born, or rather reborn a Dhyâni, still more perfect than he was before he launched forth as a Monad on the newly built chain of worlds. — (*The Secret Doctrine*, Vol. 2, p. 257.)

IX

THE DESCENT OF MANAS

WE must refer once more to the most important event in the history of the evolution of Humanity on our planet, the lighting of the flame of *Manas*, or Mind, the descent of the real Higher Ego, which made the "senseless" Monad encased in its vestures of substance into the complete Man — the *Thinker* — ready to " run the race." The development of the human shadowy vehicle, overshadowed or inspired by the energizing force of the Monad, has been touched upon slightly. As time passed, the lunar and other spiritual forces built up denser forms in harmony with the new conditions of thickening, manifesting in the different Rounds and "globes," until in the midway period, on "globe" D of the Fourth Round or present Earth, the descent of the spiritual Hierarchy of the Higher Manas, the self-conscious Intelligence, takes place, and man becomes the seven-principled being of today, although the higher Manas (the "Transcendental Self" of Du Prel,* a German philosopher who has not succumbed to the sophistries of materialism) is hardly known yet except through its emanation, the brain-mind.

The Monad is not conscious in *our* meaning of that word until it links with the Mânasic or human thinking principle. The Monad is Âtmâ-Buddhi,† and is One in essence throughout the universe; as it is the One Flame of which each of us is a Spark, the meaning of universal brotherhood being a fact in Nature becomes clear. Brotherhood is a fact waiting to be recognized; not to be artificially made. In one sense the Monad becomes individualized as the Higher Manas unites it with the physical vehicle, but in its essence it remains a part of the whole like the drop in the ocean. The Third Race of rudimentary mankind in the Fourth Round on "globe" D (our Earth),

---

* *Philosophie der Mystik.*

† See Manual No. 2.

over which the Monad brooded, gradually received the reincarnating Egos, spoken of in *The Secret Doctrine* as the "Heart of the Dhyân-Chohanic body," the hierarchy of semidivine spiritual intelligences that had been preparing in other worlds to incarnate in the Monadic vehicles forming. Some "projected a spark" (of intelligence) only, others incarnated fully. There was no need for them to pass through the primitive stages through which the Monad was energizing into form the complex vehicles they required. With the appearance of the Higher Egos, a portion of whose light gives us our ordinary intellect (for we are not yet endowed with the full consciousness of the Mânasic principle) the separation of the race into sex, with its involved problems, and the present conditions, gradually came into being. This was over 18 millions of years ago, and a mere outline of the history of man since that period requires a Manual to itself.*

The Monad or Jiva, as said in *Isis Unveiled*,

---

* Manual No. 18, *Sons of the Firemist*.

Vol. I, p. 302, is, first of all, shot down by the law of Evolution into the lowest form of matter — the mineral. After a sevenfold gyration encased in the stone (or that which will become mineral and stone in the Fourth Round) it creeps out of it, say, as a lichen. Passing thence, through all the forms of vegetable matter, into what is termed animal matter, it has now reached the point in which it has become the germ, so to speak, of the animal, that will become the physical man. All this, up to the Third Round, is formless, as matter, and senseless, as consciousness . . . this conscious, rational, individual Soul (*Manas*), "the principle, or the intelligence, of the Elohim," to receive which, he has to eat of the fruit of Knowledge from the Tree of Good and Evil. How is he to obtain all this? The Occult doctrine teaches that while the monad is cycling on downward into matter, these very Elohim — or Pitris, the lower Dhyân-Chohans — are evolving *pari passu* with it on a higher and more spiritual plane, descending also relatively into matter on their own plane of consciousness, when, after having reached a certain point, they will meet the incarnating senseless monad, encased in the lowest matter, and blending the two potencies, Spirit and Matter, the union will produce that terrestrial symbol of the "Heavenly Man" in space — PERFECT MAN.—(*The Secret Doctrine*, Vol. I, p. 246.)

Enough has been said to show that Theosophy has little sympathy with the one-sided theory of the Darwinians, for their hypothesis does not recognize some of the greatest factors in the case, such as the complexity of man's nature, the existence of an astral form within the physical, the Higher Transcendental Ego, or Manas, and the over-shadowing Âtmâ-Buddhi, all of which must be taken into consideration before any theory of evolution can be anything but imperfect. Theosophy looks on man as a spiritual being with a triple evolution — physical (including emotional and astral), Mânasic or Intellectual, and Spiritual or Monadic — and science has only partially traced the physical, the least important.

It should be clear from what has been sketched in the preceding chapters that Theosophy repudiates the abhorrent notion of the possibility of the real Man, the Manas, the re-incarnating Ego, overshadowed by the Monadic Light of Âtmâ-Buddhi, entering the body of a beast or insect. There is a possibility of the withdrawal of the light of the Higher Triad,

Âtmâ-Buddhi-Manas, from the lower personal
man as the result of many lives of utter selfishness; and also that the consciousness of the
lower Ego, like the bodily frame, will gradually decompose, though more slowly and with
infinite pain, possibly after many degrading incarnations in human form; but this in no way
implies rebirth as a pig or a monkey. As
H. P. Blavatsky says, there is the impassable
abyss of Mentality and Self-consciousness between man and the animal.*

Evolution having brought *Manas* the Thinker and
Immortal Person on to this plane, cannot send him
back to the brute which has not Manas.—(*William
Q. Judge*)

---

* See quotation on page 55 above.

X

LUNAR INFLUENCE PERSISTS

HAVING gotten a general idea of the Rounds, a little more attention can be given with profit to the curious and very important question of the transfer of life from the moon to the earth. As the newly forming center of equilibrium, which ultimately became the solid earth, drew this life to it, and the lower forms of consciousness or vestures of the Monad obtained greater solidity, the "atoms" composing them were busy assimilating the new conditions, which were higher than those they had experienced in the similar "globes" of the lunar chain. By the time the spiritual Manas, which is the real Ego of man, had incarnated at the midway period of the Fourth (our present) Round, the *habits* or cyclic impressions derived from the conditions of lunar existence had largely faded out under the fresh circumstances of earth-life; but there are still some left which are a mystery to science, and which it has never made the slightest effort to solve, hardly even to face. Such are the various periods in human and animal life which bear a direct and unmistakable relation to the changes of the moon. In diseases the crisis, as a rule, comes at intervals of seven, fourteen or twenty-one days, and other physiological periodic events are governed by the lunar cycles. In lunacy the new and full moons are critical times; in the growth and generation of insects the seven day period is well marked; in the changes of the weather the farmers persist in declaring, in spite of the scepticism of science, that the moon is the regulator.

Further information on this interesting subject is given in *Isis Unveiled* and *The Secret Doctrine,* but a new confirmation of the Theosophical knowledge must not be omitted here. The life history of the *Palolo viridis* worm of Polynesia, etc. has been known for some time to be very remarkable. It keeps accurate *lunar time!* The *Encyclopaedia Britannica* says:

About three o'clock on the morning following the third quartering of the October moon they invariably appear on the surface of the water; . . . soon after the sun rises they begin to break, and by 9 o'clock A. M. they have disappeared. The morning following the third quartering of the November moon they again appear in the same manner but in smaller quantities. After that they are not seen till October of the next year. They appear thus to deposit their ova. . . . Year by year these creatures appear according to lunar time.

Thinking that the tides might have something to do with this extraordinary phenomenon, the observers at the Carnegie Institution's Marine Laboratory at the Tortugas, in 1907, tried the experiment of putting some of the *Palolo* worms into tanks of still water. Under these conditions, *if exposed to the light of the moon*, at the third quarter nearest the summer solstice, which is the period they keep in the Gulf of Mexico, the performance took place precisely as usual; but if the moonlight was shut off they remained quiescent at the bottom of the water, and if the eggs were liberated six hours even before the proper lunar cycle they would not fructify. Evidences like this are precisely what we should expect as the lingering remains of the influence of the former life in the Lunar Chain. The *Palolo* worm is a very simple organism and has probably changed very little since its first ethereal shadowy progenitor passed over from our satellite — satellite now perhaps, but parent then.

There are other peculiarities connected with the moon, such as the shape of its orbit, which is not a cycloidal curve, like the paths of other satellites, but is concave to the position of the sun; and the comparatively close approximation in size between the diameters of the earth and moon as compared with the great disproportion between the sizes of the other satellites and their primaries — peculiarities that have caused some astronomers to advance the hypothesis that the moon is a companion planet to the earth, and not a satellite, a view much more in harmony with Theosophical records.

XI

RÉSUMÉ AND CONCLUSION

LOOKING back at the great world-periods called Rounds, we see taking place under the evolutionary push of the Monad a gradual change and development in primitive ethereal substance which had gained all the experience possible in the Lunar Chain. The Monad having left the seventh "globe" of the Lunar Chain, after a period of repose commences to energize the higher evolution of the Terrestrial Chain in its most ethereal state, a state and a process of activity that have not been fully given out by the Teachers who have possession of the exact details. We should certainly not be able to understand the conditions of those early times if told in words which are only suitable to the conditions of today; the understanding of such things needs the power to change our consciousness into sympathetic vibration with them, and that is not the privilege of the untrained man. Descending more and more deeply into material conditions, the " Pilgrim " finds itself ultimately in the present Fourth Round, in the present Fifth Race on "globe" D (our earth, the most material of all the states).

Humanity is at present just a little past the lowest point of the arc, and slowly commencing the climb which will carry it into heights of spiritual life infinitely transcending the greatest flights of the imagination of poet or prophet.

With each new Round new conditions of matter manifested themselves on the "globes" each time the rush of the life-wave reached them again. The next Round will manifest conditions of matter of which uninitiated mankind has no conception; and utterly unexpected and at present unimaginable conditions will become normal as the race progresses through the Sixth and Seventh Rounds, the last being highly spiritual and close to the Divine. During the process of evolution of terrestrial forms, and at a time when there were only the "unconscious" (from the intellectual standpoint) Monads, and the lower material principles, the real Ego incarnated, descending from higher realms (being a Dhyân-Chohan, or spiritual Intelligence, coming from past manvantaras), and gave the link needed to join the "unconscious" Monad with its material, semi-human forms. Then commenced the struggle for purification, for the higher to dominate the lower, and to polarize the whole complex nature of man in the direction of spiritual progress. This was the " Fall " of the angels, this was the casting of Prometheus to earth after he had stolen the divine Fire from heaven; these and many other allegories have been woven round the great fact of the descent of the " *Elohim* " or the *Mânasaputra*, the Sparks or Sons of the Universal Mind. The "coats of skins" which were made by " Jehovah " (the " Lord God ") for Adam and Eve were symbols of the final entry into physical flesh-life in this present Fourth Round, long after the experiences depicted in the earlier verses of Genesis, which are condensed accounts of the earlier Rounds and Races.

Theosophy opens our eyes to see that Earth is a very different thing from what mere outside appearance warrants. It is only our blindness that makes us believe that it is dark; it is only ignorance that allows us to fancy it is a lump of senseless clay; and if we make it a hell, that is our own fault. In reality it is a wonderful and magic place, full of mysterious profundities which we shall penetrate in time; and it is our *Home* in a very real sense. A survey of the evolution of the Races through the "globes" in their cyclic sweep, shows that the Brotherhood of Humanity is not a partial or artificial thing; and that the Law of Evolution infinitely transcends the dreams of Biology, for it reaches from the Depths to the Heights of Being. As soon as Humanity finds that there is no easy escape from earth into some fanciful heavenly pleasure-ground for an eternity of personal enjoyment, it will soon see that the wisest thing to do is to set its own house in order, and by practical altruism in act and thought change even the face of Nature, and find the true Heaven which is all about us. When this wisdom comes to the race as a whole, and Compassion has become the recognized law of life, and all the experience possible to man on earth has been gained, then it will be time for the heavens to " pass away with a great noise "; and then " the earth and the works that are therein shall be burned up" to make ready for the future Rounds, "a new heaven and a new earth wherein dwelleth righteousness."

> Stronger than earth has ever seen; the veil
> Is rending and the voices of the day
>   Are heard across the voices of the Dark.
> No sudden heaven, nor sudden hell for man,
>   .   .   .   .
> Aeonian evolution, swift or slow,
>   Through all the spheres — an ever opening height,
> An ever lessening earth . . .—*Tennyson*

THEOSOPHICAL

MANUALS

XVIII

SONS OF THE FIREMIST

A STUDY OF MAN

The Aryan Theosophical Press
Point Loma, California
1908

O

THEOSOPHICAL MANUALS

XVIII

SONS OF THE FIREMIST

A STUDY OF MAN

BY

A STUDENT

The Aryan Theosophical Press
Point Loma, California
1908

PREFACE

THE remarks under this head are intended to be introductory to each of the Manuals. First, as to the spirit in which they are offered. These Manuals are not written in a controversial spirit, nor as an addition to the stock of theories awaiting public approval. The writers have no time to waste in arguing with people who do not wish to be convinced, or who ridicule everything which is new to their limited outlook. Their message is for those who desire to know — those who are seeking for something that will solve their doubts and remove their difficulties. For such, all that is needed is a clear exposition of the Theosophical teachings; for they will judge of the truth of a teaching by its power to answer the questions they ask. People realize, much more now than in the early days of the Theosophical Society, the value of Theosophy;

for the ever-increasing difficulties engendered by selfishness and materialism, by doubt and the multiplicity of theories, have created an urgent demand which it alone can satisfy.

Again, it is necessary to state clearly and emphatically the genuine teachings of Theosophy, as given by the Founder of the Theosophical Society, H. P. Blavatsky, and her successors, William Q. Judge and Katherine Tingley. For, as H. P. Blavatsky predicted, there are persons who have sought to pervert these teachings and turn them into a source of profit to themselves and their own selfish and ambitious schemes. The true teachings do not lend themselves to such purposes; their ideals are of the purest and most unselfish. Hence these persons have sought to promulgate under the name of Theosophy a perverted form of the teachings, from which Brotherliness and other pure motives are omitted, and which contains doctrines which H. P. Blavatsky showed to be maleficent and destructive. As these pseudo-Theosophists have gained a certain amount of notoriety by using the names of the Theosophical Society and its Leaders, it is necessary to warn the public against them

and their misrepresentations. Their teachings
can easily be shown, by comparison, to be directly contrary to those of H. P. Blavatsky,
whom they nevertheless profess to follow. Instead of having for their basis self-sacrifice,
self-purification and the elevation of the human race, these teachings too often pander to
ambition, vanity and curiosity. In many cases
they are altogether ridiculous, and only calculated to make people laugh. Nevertheless,
as these travesties have served to discredit the
name of Theosophy and to keep earnest inquirers away from the truth, it is well that the
public should know their nature and origin.
They are the work of people who were at one
time members of the Theosophical Society,
but who did not find in it that food for their
own personalities of which they were really in
search. So they turned against their teachers
in wounded pride and vanity, and started little
societies of their own — with themselves at
the head.

The writers of these Manuals have no personal grievance against any such calumniators.
Inspired by a profound love of the sublime
teachings of Theosophy, they have made it

their life-work to bring the benefits which they have thereby received within the reach of as many people as possible. And they feel that they will have the hearty sympathy and co-operation of the public in exposing folly and bringing the truth to light.

Theosophy strikes unfamiliar ground in modern civilization, because it does not come under any particular one of the familiar headings of Religion, Science, Philosophy, etc. into which our age has divided its speculative activities. It dates back to a period in the history of mankind when such distinctions did not exist, but there was one Gnosis or Knowledge embracing all. Religion and Science, as we have them today, are but imperfect growths springing from the remnants of that great ancient system, the Wisdom-Religion, which included all that we now know as religion and science, and much more. Hence Theosophy will not appeal to the same motives as religion and science. It will not offer any cheap and easy salvation or put a premium upon mental inactivity and spiritual selfishness. Neither can it accomodate itself to the rules laid down by various schools of modern thought as to

what constitutes proof and what does not.
But it can and does appeal to the Reason.
The truth of doctrines such as Theosophy
maintains, can only be estimated by their
ability to solve problems and by their harmony
with other truths which we know to be true.
But in addition to this we have the testimony
of the ages, which has been too long neglected
by modern scholarship, but which is now being
revealed by archaeologists and scholars, as
H. P. Blavatsky prophesied that it would in
this century.

It may perhaps be as well also to remind
those who would criticise, that the state of
modern opinion is scarcely such as to warrant
anybody in assuming the attitude of a judge.
It would be quite proper for a Theosophist,
instead of answering questions or attempting
to give proofs, to demand that his questioners
should first state their own case, and to be
himself the questioner. The result would certainly show that Theosophy, to say the very
least, stands on an equal footing with any
other view, since there is no certain knowledge, no satisfying explanation, to be found
anywhere.

Since the days when the wave of materialism swept over the world, obliterating the
traces of the ancient Wisdom-Religion and
replacing it by theological dogmatism our religions have had nothing to offer us in the way
of a philosophical explanation of the laws of
Being as revealed in Man and in Nature.
Instead we have only had bare statements
and dogmatic assertions. The higher nature
of man is represented by such vague words
as Spirit and Soul, which have little or no
meaning for the majority. The laws of the
universe are briefly summed up under the
term " God," and all further consideration of
them shut off. Then came a reaction against
the dogmatism of religion, and man pinned
his faith to knowledge gained by study and
reflection, limiting his researches however to
the outer world as presented by the senses,
and fearing to trench upon the ground which
dogmatic theology had rendered the field of
so much contention. The result of this has
been that neither in religions nor sciences,
have we any teaching about the higher nature of man or the deeper mysteries of the
universe. This is a field which is left entirely

unexplored, or is at best the subject of tentative and unguided conjectures.

Until, therefore, religious teachers have something definite, consistent, and satisfactory to offer, and until science can give us something better than mere confessions of nescience or impudent denials with regard to everything beyond its own domain, Theosophy can afford to assume the rôle of questioner rather than that of questioned, and does not *owe* anybody any explanations whatever. It is sufficient to state its tenets and let them vindicate themselves by their greater reasonableness; and any further explanation that may be offered is offered rather from goodwill than from any obligation.

Theosophy undertakes to explain that which other systems leave unexplained, and is, on its own special ground, without a competitor. It can issue a challenge to theology, science, and other modern systems, to surpass it in giving a rational explanation of the facts of life.

Again, there are some questions which it is beyond the reach of the human mind, in *its present stage of development*, to answer; and it would scarcely be just to arraign Theo-sophy for not answering these.

Judgment should in all cases be preceded by careful study. There are always those who will impatiently rush to questions which a further study would have rendered unnecessary; and it is safe to say that the majority of "objections" raised to Theosophical teachings are such as could have been solved by the objector himself, had he been a genuine student. In the ordinary courses of education, scholars are required and are content, to accept provisionally many of the teacher's statements, in full confidence that further study will explain what in the beginning cannot be made clear. In the same spirit an earnest student of Theosophy will be wise enough to hold many of his difficulties in reserve, until, by further investigation, he has gained better acquaintance with his subject. In the case of those who are not willing to adopt these wise and patient methods of study, it may be reasonably questioned whether they are the more anxious to learn or to disprove.

Above all it is sought to make these Man-

uals such that they shall appeal to the heart and not *merely* to the head; that they shall be of practical service to the reader in the problems of his daily life, and not mere intel- lectual exercises. For there have been in past days books written by persons more dis- tinguished for a certain grade of mental nim- bleness than for heartfelt devotion to the cause of truth; and these have appealed only to those people who love intricate philosophi- cal problems better than practical work. But as H. P. Blavatsky so frequently urged, the message of Theosophy is for suffering human- ity; and the great Teachers, whose sole pur- pose is to bring to mankind the Light of Truth and the saving grace of real Brother- liness can have no interest in catering for the mental curiosity of merely a few well- to-do individuals. Even soulless men, said H. P. Blavatsky, can be brilliantly intellectual; but for those who are in earnest in their de- sire to reach the higher life intellectual fire- works alone will have little attraction. We intend, therefore, to keep the practical aspect of the teachings always to the front, and to show, as far as possible, that they are what

they claim to be — the gospel of a new hope and salvation for humanity.

These Booklets are not all the product of a single pen, but are written by different Students at the International Headquarters of the UNIVERSAL BROTHERHOOD AND THEOSOPHICAL SOCIETY at Point Loma, California. Each writer has contributed his own quota to the series.

For further explanations on Theosophy generally, the reader is referred to the Book List published elsewhere in this volume and to the other Manuals of this series, which treat of Theosophy and the various Theosophical teachings.

CONTENTS

I

INTRODUCTORY

THAT there has once been a Golden Age is the universal tradition of mankind. This belief is one of those larger factors in life which have either been neglected utterly or treated in the most prosaic manner as baseless myths created by a fond imagination. But a new spirit of inquiry is spreading in the world and even some of the leading thinkers in science have become dissatisfied with the contempt hitherto shown for the antique tradition. The Theosophical Movement has already had a large share in awakening a healthy skepticism in the infallibility of the purely materialistic conception of the origins of mankind, a conception which would limit the existence of rational man on earth to a few paltry thousands of years, and which, neglecting the existence of the soul, insists that man is no more than a highly developed beast, and not a spark of Divinity striving upward through perishable and transitory forms.

The scientific writers on Folklore and Comparative Mythology declare that their painstaking accumulation of facts concerning the beliefs and customs of the savage and civilized races of the past and present are only for the purpose of tracing and understanding the workings of the human mind in its alleged march from the " Stone Age " to the Twentieth Century. They calmly assume that the time-honored legends of the past, and all the so-called superstitions of the past and the present are either baseless or are merely the fanciful renderings of the commonest natural phenomena, and that for anyone to imagine there is any real wisdom in them which we do not know is to reduce himself to a low level of culture. To the Folklorist the myths, etc., are of no importance except to the extent that they give material for building up his commonplace theories. He believes in no gods; to his unpoetic mind Nature is soulless.

Theosophy proves the error of this. The Theosophist is very little interested in the contortions of the savage mind in its efforts to preserve the vestiges of truth in its possession; he is employed in finding the truth behind the forms, so as to be better able to help humanity to progress on intelligent lines. Theosophy knows and is pointing out the pearls of truth hidden under the mass of rubbish that has grown up throughout the ages.

A feeling has arisen in the hearts of thousands that there is something vitally important in the traditions of the ancients, and that they were not all deluded fools; but the materialistic interpretation of the Bible that the orthodox theologians have forced upon the world, with its literal hell and its absurd chronology, its unjust "plan of salvation" and false science, still arouses prejudice not only against the veracity of the Biblical allegories but also against those of the Sacred Scriptures of India, Chaldaea, etc.

It is not possible in the limited space at our

disposal to give the full reasons why Theoso-
.phists accept the assertions that there were
vast prehistoric civilizations ages before the
supposed Flood of Noah or the hypothetical
" Stone Age " of archaeology; it is sufficient
to mention that H. P. Blavatsky brought the
key to the strange and not always beautiful
narratives in the ancient records. Her great
work, *The Secret Doctrine,* to quote her own
words:

Asserts that a system, known as the WISDOM-
RELIGION, the work of generations of adepts and
seers, the sacred heirloom of pre-historic times —
actually exists, though hitherto preserved in the
greatest secrecy by the present Initiates; and it
points to various corroborations of its existence to
this very day, to be found in ancient and modern
works. . . . No *new* philosophy is set up in *The
Secret Doctrine,* only the hidden meaning of some
of the religious allegories of antiquity is given,
light being thrown on these by the esoteric sciences,
and the common source is pointed out, whence all
the world-religions and philosophies have sprung
. . . its doctrines and sciences which form an integral cycle of universal cosmic facts and metaphysical axioms and truths, represent a complete

and unbroken system; and that he who is brave and persevering enough, ready to crush the *animal* in himself, and, forgetting the human *self*, sacrifices it to his Higher Ego, can always find his way to become initiated into these mysteries.*

Referring students to the remarkable evidences given in *The Secret Doctrine* and *Isis Unveiled* of the accuracy of the fragments preserved under the strange Biblical, Purânic, and other accounts of the creations and destructions of the world, which read in the light of Theosophy, give a coherent story, we will pass on to our subject, the experience of humanity during the aeons of time that have elapsed while our present complex nature has been forming. The word experience is used advisedly, for the immortal principle in man, in its pilgrimage towards divinity, identifies itself with various states of existence, including numerous degrees of materiality, and endures many outward changes of earthly conditions each of which provides different opportunities for advancement.

* "The Babel of Modern Thought," *Lucifer*, 1901.

Man has not been confined to his materially embodied state on the planet Earth from the outset; he has existed upon other planes of being, more subtle than the terrestrial as we know it now, not in a supposed " supernatural " heaven, but under conditions as normal in their cycle as the physical is today. Why should there be anything extraordinary in this idea? If, as all but agnostics and materialists believe, it is possible to exist after death, minus the body, and in a condition absolutely invisible to our five senses, why should there be anything unreasonable in the Theosophical teaching that ages ago humanity gained needed experience in conditions far more ethereal than those prevailing in this corner of the universe now? The earth was certainly far more gaseous in its nature at one time; why should we not have been formed then in harmony with the environment?

Theosophy teaches that in gaining the vast experiences already stored up in the memory of the soul, mankind has traveled many roads, developing certain faculties during one cycle, and others when that cycle had run its course. The bald notion that man is merely a highly organized animal, a *Primate* with a more complex brain, who has descended in a straight line from some primeval amoeba through reptile and mammal, does not explain the mystery of his nature. All honor must be given to Darwin, Wallace, Huxley, and the indefatigable school of evolutionists for breaking down the literal misinterpretation of Genesis, but the danger of materialism has become so great that it is time the Theosophical interpretation should be understood, for it shows there is no real conflict between true science and true religion, because they are one.

II

WHAT IS MAN?

MAN is far more than he knows. He thinks he is the ordinary thinking, talking and eating, loving and hating, sinning and suffering personality of everyday life; but that is only the merest fraction of the real man; that is not the Being to whom Jesus said, " Ye are gods." Materialism says mind is a " by-product of the brain," but Theosophy shows that the brain-mind is, in a very profound sense, a " by-product " of the Higher immortal Mind, the Reincarnating Ego, the " Man for whom the hour shall never strike."*

But " still it moves," and recent observations have persuaded many Western thinkers that there are really profound depths in man hitherto entirely unsuspected by them. Strange powers of memory under hypnosis, thought-

---

* *Voice of the Silence.*

transference, clairvoyance, movement of objects without physical contact at will, etc., — things which are little more than feeble reflections of the real powers latent in man — have forced themselves upon the few independent thinkers, and have proved that behind the ordinary faculties, the five senses and the everyday mind, there lies a region totally unexplored by Western science.

But this vast region, the domain of the reincarnating Ego, is well known to the psychologists of the inner schools of the East, and Theosophy brings actual knowledge of the nature of man.

The first thing we have to learn is that the evolution of the higher central nature has been carried on through enormous ages of time separately from the evolution of the lower principles — the passional nature, the body, and the astral (or *model*) body.* The real man, the Higher Ego, knows these things, for it has lived through ages of experience, and has knowledge far transcending that of the lower

* See Manual No. 2, *Seven Principles of Man.*

man, the physical personality. The Higher
Ego knows so much more than the lower,
which has only been in existence for the short
period of one life-cycle, that it recognizes
what experiences are necessary for its real
evolution, though they may not be always
pleasing to the lower personality, Mr. A., or
Mrs. B., which resents the apparently unjust
blows of fate. But after death the withdrawal
of the best part of the lower — the spiritual
"aroma" of the past memories — into the
Higher permanent Ego allows it to perceive
that a great plan, like a silver thread, had been
running through the events of the past life.
Then as the lower nature becomes purified
the "threshold of sensation" broadens, until
when absolute impersonality is gained we shall
know ourselves as we are, and realize the full
continuity of purpose through the labyrinth
of past lives.

A few independent psychologists of America
and Europe have satisfied themselves that besides the "objective mind," as they call the
brain-personality of ordinary waking life,

there is something, a "subjective mind," possessing higher powers; but their "subjective
mind" is not the Higher Ego, for it can be
hypnotized and deceived with ease. It is merely the manifestation of qualities of some of
the "sheaths" or subdivisions of the astral
body which are brought into action when the
physical senses are paralysed, either through
abnormal cataleptic conditions or by the haz-
ardous practice of hypnotism. These sheaths
of the astral body are possessed of remarkable
powers, the result of processes of evolution
extending over long periods. The astral body,
though capable of displaying these powers is
not to be considered a spiritual being; its
consciousness is largely automatic and its co-
hesion breaks up soon after death in normal
cases. When the terrible bondage of personality — that egotism whose strength is hardly
suspected until the candidate for purification
sets about its destruction in serious earnest —
is broken, the astral principles will be at the
service of the perfect man, but the attempt
to arouse them artificially by hypnotic sugges-

tion or other abnormal means is fraught with extreme danger to life or sanity. The ancient philosophers who were initiated into the Mysteries and who thoroughly studied the principles of man, and *knew their origin,* took precautions against the errors and dangers arising from hypnotic suggestion which are unknown to the amateur modern researcher who has received no training in the Esoteric schools. While these modern investigators who have made a few tentative efforts to investigate the lower psychic phenomena are playing with shells on the ocean beach of psychology, the adepts have sounded its depths and know its secrets and its dangers, and the long, self-sacrificing, and impersonal preparations required, before it can be safely traversed.

Speaking of the origins of man's complex and mixed nature H. P. Blavatsky says:

. . . Man was not created the complete being he is now, however imperfect he still remains. There was a spiritual, a psychic, an intellectual, and an animal evolution, from the highest to the lowest, as well as a physical development — from the simple and homogeneous, up to the more complex and heterogeneous; though not quite on the lines traced for us by the modern evolutionists. This double evolution in two contrary directions, required various ages, of diverse natures and degrees of spirituality and intellectuality, to fabricate the being now known as man. Furthermore, the one absolute, ever acting and never erring law, which proceeds on the same lines from one eternity (or Manvantara) to the other — ever furnishing an ascending scale for the manifested, or that which we call the great Illusion (*Mahâ-Mâyâ*), but plunging Spirit deeper and deeper into materiality on the one hand, and then *redeeming it through flesh* and liberating it — this law, we say, uses for these purposes the Beings from other and higher planes, men or *Minds* (Manus) in accordance with their Karmic exigencies.*

---

* *The Secret Doctrine,* vol. ii, page 87.

III

CYCLIC PROGRESS

THOUGH Nature's curves of activity appear circular when surveyed from one point of view, they are really spirals which never pass over the same ground twice. So the evolution of man, which is the most important event on our planet (for all tends to become self-conscious, or Man), proceeds through a spiral progress upon our Earth-chain of globes, and more particularly, upon the many different states of existence through which our world has passed.

The uniformity of plan in Nature's methods in great and small things, is strikingly exemplified by the similarity of the general scheme of evolution guiding the Universal or Kosmic, the Planetary, and the Human development. The principle is firstly that the Divine Impulse causes the universe to manifest periods or ages of alternate activity and repose, — or what seems repose in comparison with the intensity of life during the *"Manvantara,"* as the objective or active condition is called; and secondly, that as the *" Pralaya,"* or subjective repose, reaches it close, the objective world is called into being and proceeds from the highest spiritual states down in regular degrees to and through the densest materiality, and then back again to the original condition plus the experience gained on the vast pilgrimage.

The smaller cycles within the great Journey are spiral curves, each one of which consists of still smaller spirals until at last the individual life of man is reached. Each single life on earth is but a part of the smallest spiral; the rest of the curve is traced in more ethereal states. The reincarnating Ego, the real Man, descends for incarnation from the spiritual condition of " Devachan " * through denser " astral " conditions to physical earth-life, during which it passes through a regular series

* See Manual No. 6, *Kâmaloka and Devachan.*

of phases; then at death it returns through the astral, semi-material conditions to the spiritual peace and rest of Devachan. This continues life after life until there is no further need of experience in that cycle, and, the greater spiral being rounded, a new path is entered.

There are seven great circuits called " Rounds " in the journey of the *Monad* or Ray of Divinity which ultimately becomes Man, during which it assumes many bodies and passes through many vicissitudes of which ordinary history has no conception. The succession of the " Globe-conditions " under which this journey has proceeded, and during which man has obtained present self-consciousness, is outlined in the preceding Manual (No. 17). During the First, Second, and Third Rounds, the Monad descended into matter, and in the Fifth, Sixth, and Seventh it will be traveling upward. We are in the middle or Fourth Round, during which we have gained full self-consciousness, and now the real fight of the Higher nature for supremacy has commenced. We read in *The Secret Doctrine:*

Starting upon the long journey immaculate; descending more and more into sinful matter, and having connected himself with every atom in manifested *Space* — the *Pilgrim,* having struggled through and suffered in every form of life and being, is only at the bottom of the valley of matter, and half through his cycle, when he has identified himself with collective Humanity. This, *he has made in his own image.* In order to progress upwards and homewards, the "God" has now to ascend the weary uphill path of the Golgotha of Life. It is the martyrdom of self-conscious existence. Like Viśvakarman he has to sacrifice *himself to himself* in order to redeem all creatures, to resurrect from the many into the *One Life.* Then he ascends into heaven indeed; where, plunged into the incomprehensible absolute Being and Bliss of Paranirvâna, he reigns unconditionally, and whence he will redescend again at the next "coming," which one portion of humanity expects in its dead-letter sense as the *second advent,* and the other as the last "Kalki Avatâr." *

---

* *The Secret Doctrine,* vol. I, page 268.

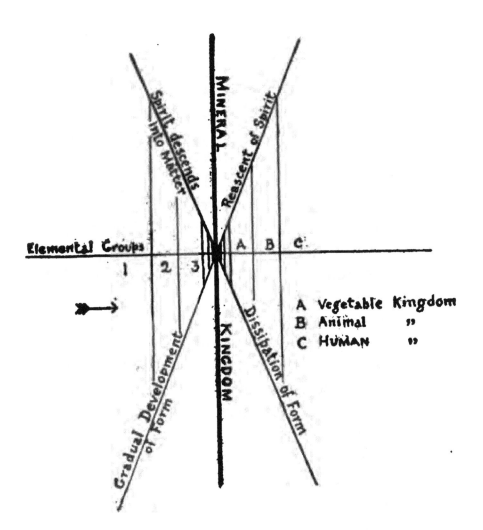

Although we are in the middle or "lowest" globe-condition of the Fourth, or lowest circuit of the spiral journey, we are not exactly midway in the Rounds. The present "globe," D, provides conditions for the evolution of seven great human races to succeed each other upon it, and we are now well on in the Fifth of these human races. As the *Fourth Race* is the most material (corresponding with the Fourth *Round*) it is clear that we have passed the center, but as nearly all the work preceding the Fourth Round, and a good deal of that of the early part of the Fourth Round, was merely preparatory building up of the being now complete as man, we are not very far on in our career as self-conscious responsible beings. The great battle, the final "moment of choice" between spirituality and materiality (the victory of the latter resulting in ultimate loss of the soul) will not arrive until the Fifth Round, but every act of today is a preparation for that critical period.

In the development of the unborn infant we find a perfect example of the repetition or reflection of the great plan of evolution in little. As its body is being built up by invisible forces in readiness for the incarnation of the immortal Ego all the conditions of the past history of mankind are repeated in miniature, and in order. This will be referred to again; it is mentioned here as an illustration of Nature's principle of correspondences, of reflecting the great in the small. The development and decay of the races, nations, and individuals on each " globe," repeat the broad outline presented in the Cosmic system which includes the minor periods in its scope. The current of the life-wave passes through conditions of greater and greater limitation and less and less spirituality called " globes," as it descends along the First Round of the great spiral, but as they are extremely difficult for us to understand, very little is said about them until the present globe " D " of the Fourth Round is reached.

William Q. Judge very clearly expresses the succession of the races on Earth (globe " D ") during the Fourth Round:

The appearance of these great root-races is always just when the world's development permits. When the globe was forming, the first root-race was more or less ethereal and had no such body as we now inhabit. The cosmic environment became more dense and the second race appeared, soon after which the first wholly disappeared. Then the third came on the scene, after an immense lapse of time, during which the second had been developing the bodies needed for the third. At the coming of the fourth root-race it is said that the present human form was evolved, although gigantic and in some respects different from our own. It is from this point — the fourth race — that the Theosophical system begins to speak of man as such.

In the archaic *Book of Dzyan,* quoted in *The Secret Doctrine,* it is said that " The first race on every zone was moon-colored; the second, yellow like gold; the third, red; the fourth, brown, which became black with sin."*

The present inhabitants of the earth are composed of relics of the later Third and the Fourth Races and of the present great Fifth Race, of which America is producing the latest branch or sub-race.

---

* *The Secret Doctrine,* vol. II, page 227.

IV

THE SPARK AND THE FLAME

THE Theosophical system differs from the popular scientific speculations of the day chiefly in its positive assertion, and demonstration in practice, that man is in reality an evolving soul traveling a well-defined path, and wearing down many physical bodies in its journey towards divinity.

Materialistic science limits human consciousness to the transient interaction of perishable brain-cells; it gives no particle of light on the past or the future of each unit; it repudiates the pre-existence of the soul, and regards everything subsequent to embodied earth-life as unknowable or non-existent — a curious commentary upon the efforts of the centuries of " dogmatic theology "! Science regards the race as the only unit of progress; the individual being supposed to be as ephem-

eral as the " beasts that perish," and his existence entirely subordinate to that of the race
— which itself will perish utterly when the
sun grows cold !

But Theosophy, while admitting that the
race as a whole is on the upward way —
though not without many set-backs and fail-
ures — follows the progress of the " Monad,"
the Ray of the One Divine Existence, which
incarnates over and over again in every condition within the terrestrial environment, until,
after being united with the real thinking Ego,
the Higher Manas or " Human Soul," it has
exhausted the possibilities of the great cycle
through which it has to pass. Then it is trans-
ported to another garden of the Law to proceed on a still higher evolution of which we
cannot have any conception at present.

Darwinian Evolution ignores the " Thread-
soul " running through the consecutive exist-
ences of man ; it gives no light on what it is
that evolves ; it confuses the immortal man of
the past and future with his perishable body.
Theosophy, on the other hand, offers a clear

picture of the eternal progression of all Nature up to higher states of consciousness, like the mathematical line which continually approaches another but never meets it though prolonged to infinity. Theosophy does not fall into the theological fallacy that every man at birth is a newly created soul whose acts in one brief life are destined to make or mar its whole future for eternity.

The " Monad," the immortal being, cannot be called *a* spirit, for it is not in essence separate from the Oversoul. H. P. Blavatsky calls it a Ray of Divinity, and it is the substratum round which the astral model, which itself formed the basis for the physical, was gradually built. Ultimately the Higher Ego, the part that makes a man a man, united with the Monadic Ray, like one beam of sunshine following another through a hole, and, merging with it, gave self-consciousness.

The relationship of the Divine overshadowing Ray, "Âtmâ-Buddhi,"* with the Thinker, the Higher Ego, is difficult to understand,

---

* See Manual No. 2, *Seven Principles of Man.*

and in so brief an essay it is sufficient to
mention that the former is a universal principle manifesting through forms, but is not
humanly conscious until the Mind or Manas
assimilates it. It is the substratum of Reality,
toward the knowledge of which all evolution
tends. It is the evolutionary force imprisoned
within, and steadily pushing all things towards
higher states. For a fuller statement of this
difficult point a careful study of *The Secret
Doctrine* is necessary, but truly we need a
higher spiritual penetration than is common
today before a full understanding of it can
be gained; yet it is a logical necessity that
there should be a Ray from the Unknown
Divine Source permeating all things, countless
sparks of the One Flame. In the *Bhagavad-
Gîtâ* there are some wonderfully expressive
passages referring to the Divine Monad:

He who seeth the Supreme Being existing alike
imperishable in all perishable things, sees indeed.
. . . This Supreme Spirit, O son of Kunti, even
when it is in the body, neither acteth nor is it
affected by action, because, being without beginning

and devoid of attributes, it is changeless. . . . As a single sun illuminateth the whole world, even so doth the One Spirit illumine every body, O son of Bhârata. — (ch. xiii)

It is even a portion of myself which, having assumed life in this world of conditioned existence, draweth tógether the five senses and the mind in order that it may obtain a body and may leave it again. . . . Presiding over the eye, the ear, the touch, the taste, and the power of smelling, and also over the mind, he experienceth the objects of sense. The deluded do not see the spirit when it quitteth or remains in the body, nor when, moved by the qualities, it has experience in the world. But those who have the eye of wisdom perceive it, and devotees who industriously strive to do so see it dwelling in their own hearts, etc.—(ch. xv)

Spirit and Matter are not regarded in Theosophy as two fundamentally different things, but as two aspects of an underlying Unity, the cause of both. Once' they are launched forth into manifestation the Life-substance descends into material conditions, the interplay of the two opposite polarities produces all the phenomena of Nature, and Karma, the Law of cause and effect, comes into action.

Thus the experience is gained for which all this wonderful Evolution and Involution is set in motion.

In order to become apparent, electricity must be in the positive and negative conditions, and so it is with the Divine Unity which manifests in Matter and Spirit. When Matter and Spirit are not apparent, unknown conditions exist; between the periodic appearances of universes this Nirvânic condition prevails.

During the cyclic career of the Monad in this World-Period it requires vestures suitable to show forth its different potentialities and latent states of consciousness. To obtain these the intelligent hierarchical forces in Nature touched the springs which aroused its powers and set in motion the Building Forces inherent in it, so that model archetypal forms were gradually projected from spheres of existence where they had been waiting for the evolutionary impulse; physical molecules were finally attracted to them, clothing them with the material suitable for the grossest form of life; the emotional and intellectual faculties were aroused; and after many ages, primitive dual-sexed physical man came into being. But not *perfect* man, for humanity has not yet developed all its intellectual principles, still less the spiritual. They are all within our grasp, but we have a weary road to travel before we can stand forth as a race of Christs or Buddhas, and the first step we have to take is the practical recognition of the real inner unity or solidarity of mankind. A mere nominal assent to the principle of Universal Brotherhood, though one may be fully convinced intellectually, will not avail, except as a preliminary step; the real consciousness of the inner divine nature of man only comes by the cultivation of the finer attributes of mind and heart, such as Compassion, that urge which feels an injury to another as keenly as to oneself, that inexpressible yearning that all humanity shall cease to live this death in life; by that courage which shrinks from nothing when the interest of others is at stake; and by the purification that comes only from joyous unselfish work for others.

Now we have come across a new idea hitherto unrecognized by science but which explains many mysteries. There is a model or semi-substantial "astral" form existing in man into which the physical particles of our bodies are built, which holds them together, and which persists for some time after death. H. P. Blavatsky said that the question of the existence of this ethereal form was the only real point of difference between Theosophy and modern Science; and since she wrote things have changed in the scientific world. A large portion of it no longer denies the *possibility* of many psychic phenomena that it condemned unheard formerly, and, through the admissions which a large number of leading scientists have been compelled to make by the examination of the facts, the existence of an astral form, distinct from the physical, is becoming a matter of accepted knowledge. Once this is admitted the greatest difficulty in accepting the Theosophical teaching on many vital points, is removed. Theosophy is the only system which has been acquainted with kindred facts for ages and which has recorded their origins, and knows their significance.

But although Theosophy holds the keys of knowledge, *that does not mean they have all been given to the world.* On the contrary, the Custodians of the ancient records have withheld the greater part of their information, and have given out but the main outlines with a few details here and there; still there is more than enough for the present, and day by day fresh corroborations are coming up which enable students of Theosophy to interpret with more clearness the valuable hints that have been given.

V

THE LATENT POWERS AWAKEN

IT is now possible to go a little more into detail concerning man on "globe" D of this Fourth Round. For a general sketch of the Rounds and the position therein of "globe" D in each Round the reader is referred to the preceding Manual (No. 17), and for a wealth of evidence from innumerable records of the past history of mankind preserved in living tradition, in manuscript, on palm-leaf or papyrus, carved in glyph or symbol on enduring stone, or set forth in other ways, *Isis Unveiled* and *The Secret Doctrine* should be consulted.

The "inherent and necessary law of development" spoken of by science, is contained in the Divine Spark or Monad (Âtmâ-Buddhi). The Monad is the cause of Evolution and lies behind all minor agencies such as Natural

and Sexual Selection, etc., which are the in- -
struments through which it works for progress. The Monad, after enjoying an existence upon the "*Lunar* Chain," a condition
of existence of which the Moon is a surviving
relic, enters the Terrestrial Chain of "globes,"
clothes itself with the finer states of earthly
matter, and assumes in orderly succession various changes of consciousness unknown to modern thought, on its way to become man.

Nature's first attempts to form man were
at first unsuccessful, for the unfoldment of
the Monadic potentialities is unable to proceed beyond a certain point without the addition of another principle, the Manas, or reflecting Mind, and this had to be evoked by
Beings possessing this self-consciousness, who
had been evolving under other conditions.
They communicated to the imperfect animal
man the divine principle of intelligence, which
is not a "by-product of the brain." Endowed
with this, the rudimentary half-formed man
became truly man, a thinker, and acquired that
greater power of progression which renders

him different from the brutes, who have not had the latent intellectual and self-conscious powers of the Monad aroused. The doctrine of the coming of the " Sons of Mind " into nascent humanity is one of the greatest revelations of Theosophy, for it explains the presence of the Higher Ego in us; and though it is found in more or less veiled hints in all the world-scriptures, it was not understood until they were studied in the revealing light of Theosophy. The doctrine is concealed under " blinds " in the first chapters of *Genesis.* The reader is urged to dwell upon this supremely important point carefully, and to observe how it completely alters the point of view from which the origin and nature of man must be studied.

The various "Angels," " Gods," " Powers," and other subordinate divinities that were believed in until this materialistic age, by divers peoples, are the groups or Hierarchies of spiritual and semi-spiritual Beings, corresponding to the principles in man, which assisted the unfolding of the inherent powers of the Mon-

ad, by " projecting," so to speak, the vivifying
sparks in order to arouse the particular aspect
or principle corresponding to themselves, each
to each. One of the leading features of Theosophy, which opens a line of inquiry quite
new to modern thinkers and without which
they must continue to struggle to explain natural phenomena by means of inadequate materialistic hypotheses, is that humanity and all
things make progress by responding to stimuli
which arouse latent powers. These stimuli
can only come from more advanced intelligences who already have these particular qualities in activity. Dwell carefully upon this
fundamental concept.

THE FIRST AND SECOND RACES

WHEN incipient man arrived upon earth
at the beginning of the Fourth Round, the
Hierarchy called the " Lunar Pitris " or
Fathers, furnished him with his first dwelling,
a subtle ethereal form, the "shadow" of themselves, which afforded the elemental forces of

nature a model upon which to build. The consciousness of this highly ethereal First Race was instinctual and has gradually blended with our complex make-up so intimately that we cannot now distinguish it separately. Self-consciousness does not awaken until the end of the Third Race.

The first race of men were, then, simply the images, the astral doubles, of their Fathers, who were the pioneers, or the most progressed Entities from a preceding though *lower* sphere, the shell of which is now our Moon. . . . At the end of the Third Round, they were already human in their divine nature, and were thus called upon to become the creators of the forms destined to fashion the tabernacles of the less progressed Monads, whose turn it was to incarnate.*

After many ages this shadowy, almost in-comprehensible state of humanity — or what was to become humanity later — changed, and the First Race gave birth to the Second, and that to the Third. Of the First and Second little can be said. There was no death at first,

* *The Secret Doctrine*, vol. II, page 115.

for this incipient humanity had no physical bodies to wear out; spirit and matter were not yet equilibrized.

Even the state of mental torpor and unconsciousness of the first two Races and of the first half of the Third Race, is symbolized, in the second chapter of *Genesis*, by the *deep sleep of Adam* . . . the slumber of the Soul and Mind.*

The Primitive Race merged into the Second Race and became one with it. The "man" of the second Race, which was a little more materialized than the First, produced offspring by " fission " or " budding," in the manner of cell division. At this time, we may note, the Race was still devoid of the element of Desire and Passion, which did not evolve until the Third Race, and so hermaphroditism was the natural order.

In *The Secret Doctrine* H. P. Blavatsky published some remarkable Stanzas or Verses from an archaic MS., *The Book of Dzyan*, to which she had access, but which is not yet available to archaeologists. This antique re-

* *The Secret Doctrine*, vol. II, page 181.

cord contains a brief *résumé* of the whole history of mankind, and it is from this and similar accounts that the Biblical and other sacred books derive their allegories. The following will give an idea of the spirit of the work:

The breath [or human Monad] needed a form; The Fathers [Pitris] gave it.

The breath needed a gross body; the Earth [lower elementals] molded it.

The breath needed the Spirit of Life [Prâna]; the Solar Lhas [the vital electric principle residing in the Sun] breathed it into its form.

The breath needed a Mirror of its Body [astral shadow]. "We gave it our own," said the Dhyânis.

The Breath needed a Vehicle of Desires; "It has it," said the Drainer of Waters [the fire of passion].

But Breath needs a mind to embrace the Universe; "We cannot give that," said the Fathers. "I never had it," said the Spirit of the Earth. "The form would be consumed were I to give it mine," said the Great Fire. . . .

Man remained an empty senseless Bhûta. . . . Thus have the boneless given life to those who became men with bones in the third [Race]. *

* *The Secret Doctrine*, vol. II, page 17.

The " men, during the First and Second Races, were not physical beings, but merely *rudiments* of the future men "; the sexes had not become separated, and, above all, the descent of the *Manas,* that Spark of Divine Intelligence which transformed the (intellectually) senseless embryonic, and almost structureless sub-human forms of these Races into Men — potential Gods — had not taken place. But when "Adam" awoke from his *deep sleep* he found " Eve " beside him, and the " Fall " took place. The descent into matter, accompanied by the separation of the sexes, was thus allegorized; the material bodies being referred to in *Genesis* iii. 21, " Unto Adam also and to his wife did the Lord God make coats of skins, and clothed them." In these "coats," the primitive, astral forms which had been weaving round the Monad for countless ages, perfecting the vehicle for the Mind to use, were enclosed. The earlier ethereal evolution of the Monad through the early Rounds and the first Races of this Round, the ages of innocence, is included in the first chapter and

part of the second chapter of *Genesis*. With
the eating of the fruit of the Tree of Knowledge came personal responsibility and the
power to rise or fall intelligently. This took
place finally in the latest Third and the Fourth
or Atlantean Race.

The First and Second Races, being boneless,
and not material in the full sense of the word,
have left no traces in the rocks; their relics
have to be sought elsewhere. As the "men"
of the First Race melted away they were absorbed in the denser, though still "viscid"
forms of the Second Race, but not until the
Third Race had been established for several
millions of years, was there anything tangible
enough to last until today as a witness. The
most ethereal vestures of the Monad were
forming around it, until then in harmony with
the gradually condensing substance of the
Earth-Chain of globes: they are now to
be found *within* the human frame, but few
scientists have yet suspected the existence of
these semi-material principles, the astral bodies. The Monad cannot act directly upon the

material plane, where it is "unconscious" until it has acquired the intermediate Mânasic or Higher Intelligence or Mind, and that mind itself cannot act directly through the physical body; it also needs something more ethereal to serve as a "transformer" of the lower vibrations into higher ones which it can appreciate. This is the function of the complex system of astral and emotional (kâmic) bodies, .which were, at one period, "naked, and they were not ashamed," * for they were in harmony with the surrounding conditions. Gradually, as the Third Race developed and passed out of the sinlessness of "unconsciousness" into the strife caused by the progress of evolutionary unfoldment and the descent into matter, the physical body took shape, molded upon the primeval archetypal form.

Man, in the course of the innumerable experiences of the Monad in the early Rounds, passed through and shed many slightly varying ethereal forms which were afterwards taken up and utilized by his "younger bro-

---

* *Genesis,* ii. 25.

thers," the animals, and around or into which their physical bodies were molded. The possession of unused "rudimentary organs," like the ear-muscles, is thus clearly explained by Theosophy, for it shows that Man is the storehouse of all forms, a few of which, though unnecessary now, still give evidence of their past existence. The development of the human embryo shows the possession of many more forms than are preserved in adult life (such as gill-clefts in the neck). The unborn child runs through the whole gamut of evolution from the mineral kingdom, through the plant-form and upwards, reproducing in little the broad conditions through which the Monad has passed throughout the preceding Rounds and Races.

It may be asked, What evidence is there that an astral body is still to be found within man's physical frame? In the short space at our disposal it is impossible to quote authorities, but there is an immense mass of reliable information upon the subject which can be readily found by anyone who needs it. D'Assier's

Posthumous Humanity contains a well-digested array of cases only explicable by the existence of a fluidic body surviving the death of the material form. Professor Sir W. Crookes, Dr. Alfred R. Wallace, M. Camille Flammarion, Professor Botazzi of Naples, and others who rank among the foremost thinkers of the Twentieth century, have recorded with care their rigid scientific experiments in the demonstration of its existence, and to a limited extent, of its structure and powers. In several of the Manuals of this series the question of the Astral world is treated in the light of Theosophy, and in *Isis Unveiled* H. P. Blavatsky entered very fully into its relation to human life.

VI

INCARNATION OF THE EGO

WE have now arrived at the most important point in the history of forming humanity and one that is extremely difficult to render in simple language. While there was a Ray or Expression of the Divine in each primitive and potential human form from the very beginning, help was needed before it could advance towards *self*-consciousness. To give it this, to open the mental eye, other more progressed spiritual Beings had to overshadow or blend with the Monad, furnishing it with the needed touch to arouse the latent fires. But as H. P. Blavatsky says, "Nature unaided fails," that is to say, the efforts of the Nature-forces to create a thinking, intelligent man, merely resulted in the birth of grotesque creatures and progenitors of the animals, though these attempts were energized

by the evolutionary tendency active in the
Monadic essence, which itself is part of the
whole Kosmic movement towards higher conditions. The mysterious beings, the " Sons
of Mind," who merged their consciousness
into the incomplete forms of the Third Race
making them human, had passed through vast
experiences in other spheres but had not got
beyond the necessity of further incarnation in
matter, and they had to blend with rudimentary man before further advance could be
made.

But there are not two Monads in each
human being, for with the formation of complete man by the arousing of the latent powers
within, *he becomes a unit.* The Monad is not
a substantial entity that may be handled in
any way; though it has to be considered while
speaking in general language as an apparently
separate Ray of the Divine Oversoul, yet that
Oversoul is really One. Could we see ourselves as we really are — as a whole — we
should be greatly astonished. We should see
how the innumerable Principles or Hierar-

chies of Creators in Nature had united to
build up our complex structure, by drawing
from the inexhaustible storehouse in the Monad those qualities which enable the far-
stretching planes of Nature manifested in this
Kosmic period to be entered upon and ex-
plored in due course. Of our real make-up
the physical body is the least important and
the most ephemeral, though, of course, an absolute necessity in contacting the present physical conditions.

In the early part of the Third Race a certain proportion of the Mânasic Intelligences
entered the evolving forms, but the greater
number deferred incarnating until later. The
first were few; they became the teachers,
guides, and helpers to the later comers, who
were the larger mass of average humanity.
There was a third section who were "not
ready" at first, and they have had to put up
with inferior bodily forms which had been
degraded by evil living through ignorance, the
direct result of those Higher Egos having held
aloof from the sacrifice of the " Fall " into

material life. It is their Karma. As a consequence, we are now suffering from many evils in the world that might have been avoided.

The Secret Doctrine is very reticent concerning the exact method by which man derived his physical body after the Monad had passed through the ethereal states of the Earlier Rounds and Races. H. P. Blavatsky says:

Finally, it is shown in every ancient Scripture and Cosmogony that man evolved primarily as a *luminous incorporeal* form, over which, like molten brass round the clay model of the sculptor, the physical frame of his body was built by, through, and from, the lower forms and types of terrestrial life.*

On page 736. vol. II of *The Secret Doctrine,* the writer gives some information which must have proved startling to materialistic minds. Speaking of the " midway point of evolution," she says it is

that stage where the *astral* prototypes definitely begin to pass into the physical, and thus become subject

* *The Secret Doctrine,* vol. II, page 112.

to the differentiating agencies now operative around us. Physical causation supervenes immediately on the assumption of "coats of skins" — *i. e.,* the physiological equipment in general. . . . The known physiological contrivances in organisms [for eating, digesting, etc.] were almost entirely evolved subsequently to the incipient physicalization of the 7 Root-Types out of the astral — during the "midway halt" between the two planes of existence. . . .

As to the former reality of the descent [of the astral] into the physical, which culminated in physiological man and animal, we have a palpable testimony in the fact of the so-called spiritualistic "materializations."

In all these instances a complete temporary mergence of the astral into the physical takes place. The evolution of *physiological* Man out of the astral races of the *early* Lemurian age — the Jurassic age of Geology — is exactly paralleled by the "materialization" of "spirits" (?) in the séance room. In the case of Professor Crookes' "Katie King," the presence of a *physiological* mechanism — heart, lungs, etc. — was indubitably demonstrated!!*

There are other passages in H. P. Blavatsky's works which give more light upon this extremely important and interesting subject, but

---

* *The Secret Doctrine,* vol. II, pages 736-7.

complete information concerning the details of
the process has been reserved.   Enough has
been suggested to provide material for intelligent thought, and to show that the ape-ancestry
theory *is not the only alternative* to the special
creation Adam-and-Eve story taken literally.

With the general transformation of conditions the separation of the sexes took place.
Until then there was no duality, no male and
female, and as the present arrangement of
mammalian reproduction is not the sole method in all Nature's kingdoms even today, we
need not be surprised at the Theosophical
statement that the time will come when it
will be obsolete.   This will not be until man
has learned the great lesson of self-control
and has arrived much nearer the stature of
the Divine.   The Higher Ego is beyond the
temporary illusion of sex.

With the incarnation of the " Lords of the
Flame " — the Mind or Mânasic principle —
in their three stages of progress, the true beginning of " Man," the Thinker, is made.   This
took place about 18 millions of years ago, and

ever since then we have been complete *septen-ary* beings while on earth, experiencing the most extraordinary vicissitudes of climate, temperature, and civilization. Periods of barbarism have succeeded periods of the greatest intellectual brilliancy, the ocean has flowed over the sites of long forgotten cities, new lands have appeared many times, and mankind has had to start afresh more than once from the widespread ruin of nations and continents. There have been many destructions by water, fire, and earthquake, and the "primitive man" of the Stone Age of archaeology is not primitive at all. Long before he appeared there were magnificent civilizations, of which practically not a trace remains in recognizable form. When the time comes for the revelation of the full details of the past civilizations which existed millions of years before the so-called primitive beginnings of our present one, there will be many surprises. Of course, as we ourselves are the heritage of the past, it will be clear that we have gained such experiences in what we have passed through in

the immense period we have been on earth,
that it will not be necessary to repeat them in
the same form. Our present age is different
from every preceding one in the details of
life, even in the natural conditions.

The first Race had three *rudimentary* elements in
it; and *no fire* as yet; because, with the Ancients,
the evolution of man, and the growth and development of his spiritual and physical senses, were subordinate to the evolution of the elements on the
Cosmic plane of this Earth. . . .

The following order on parallel lines may be
found in the evolution of the Elements and the
Senses; or in Cosmic terrestrial " MAN " or " Spirit,"
and mortal physical man:

1 Ether	Hearing	Sound.
2 Air	Touch	Sound and Touch.
3 Fire, or Light	Sight	Sound, Touch and Color.
4 Water	Taste	Sound, Touch, Color and Taste.
5 Earth	Smell	Sound, Touch, Color, Taste and Smell.

As seen, each Element adds to its own characteristics, those of its predecessor; as each Root-Race
adds the characterizing sense of the preceding Race.
The same is true in the *septenary* creation of man,

who evolves gradually in seven stages, and on the same principles . .. .*

Though we have learned much which in the normal man of today is locked up in the mysterious storehouse to which the Higher Ego alone has access, and which only those who have " become one with the Father in heaven " can or dare remember, the Higher part of our being is awaiting fuller development in the future Races, the Sixth and Seventh; and for the completion of perfect Man there are the immeasurable vistas of the Fifth, Sixth, and Seventh *Rounds* stretching in front of us with their unthinkable promise of glory. The Perfected Men who are helping humanity now and always are Those who have lifted themselves, by heroic effort, above the level of ordinary mankind of this Fifth Race, into the condition which will not be normal until the next Round. Ages must pass before that period arrives, but we can hasten the good time by the study and practice of altruism.

* *The Secret Doctrine*, vol. II, page 107.

VII

LEMURIA, THE CRADLE OF MANKIND

THE development of the Third Race is re-corded in the Indian Purânas and other world-scriptures and traditions under various allegories, and its innumerable sub-races and divisions are referred to under the disguise of deities, heroes, kings, etc. The interpretations were reserved for students. The Third Race subdivides naturally into three great groups, the first of which may be called the " Sons of the Firemist." They sacrificed themselves at the beginning for the good of the Monads who were waiting their coming and failing their appearance would have had to linger on for ages in irresponsible, animal-like, though in appearance human, forms. Opposed to this lofty group came the lowest, which wandered far from the human fold at last. To the dregs of this group is attributed the origin of the anthropoid apes, of which we shall hear more later. These two groups were not the ancestors of the majority of the human race now on earth. The Higher group was very limited in numbers, and the lower was so mindless that but for later crossings with higher races it might not have persisted in human form. The race that became the majority of later mankind was intermediate between the lowest and the highest, and it was under the guidance of the highest that they developed the civilization of Lemuria, the first inhabited continent, properly so-called.

It is a most difficult thing to place the succession of the later Third (Lemurian), the Fourth (Atlantean), and the Fifth (the present or Aryan), in right relation to the geological periods, because there is nothing definitely known to Science concerning the duration of any of the ages of sedimentation. The existence of the earth in a stratified condition is variously estimated by geologists and astronomers as having endured not less than ten million years and not more than one thousand

GEOLOGICAL PERIODS		LEMURIAN	ATLANTEAN	FIFTH RACE
Cainozoic (Tertiary and Recent)	Recent Pleistocene Pleiocene Meiocene Eocene			
Mesozoic (Secondary)	Cretaceous Jurassic Triassic			
Palaeozoic	Carboniferous Devonian Silurian Cambrian			
Primary	Archaean			

million, and as we have not the slightest evidence of the rate of sedimentation in the far distant ages there is nothing to prove definitely which small division corresponds with the Races and sub-Races whose records we are considering. The above diagram represents, with no attempt at positive accuracy, the parallelism.

The continent of Lemuria (a name invented

by Science and adopted by Theosophy for public use in lieu of its own term) extended across the Indian Ocean and far on both sides of it. To the Northwest it stretched as far as Sweden and Norway. The great English fresh-water deposit called the Wealden — which every geologist regards as the estuary of a former great river — is the bed of the main stream which drained Northern Lemuria in the Secondary age. Towards the East it included New Zealand, Australia, and the Pacific Islands, and even a strip of California including Point Loma. The Pacific Islands are the remains of mountain summits belonging to this submerged region. Easter Island (110° W., 26° S.) contains remarkable gigantic statues, enduring witnesses to the artistic ability and mechanical skill of the later Lemurians. H. P. Blavatsky gives a few outlines of the primitive civilizations which slowly grew up through the efforts of the later Third Race men. She speaks of —

men and civilized nations, not Palaeolithic savages only; who, under the guidance of their *divine* Rulers,

built large cities, cultivated arts and sciences, . . .
This primeval civilization did not, as one may think,
immediately follow their physiological transformation. Between the final evolution and the first city
built, many hundred thousands of years had passed.
Yet, we find the Lemurians in their sixth sub-race
building their first rock cities out of stone and lava.
One of such great cities of primitive structure was
built entirely of lava, some thirty miles west from
where Easter Island now stretches its narrow piece
of sterile ground, and was entirely destroyed by a
series of volcanic eruptions.*

The Lemurians of the last ages were now
complete men; in fact they had perceptive
powers that have become practically atrophied
since. They had physical bodies which repro-
duced their kind in present fashion. Between
the sketch-humanity of the First and Second
Races and the full development of the latest
Third, Nature tried several modes of reproduction, and many offshoot and degraded races
had come into being, but gradually the human
stock settled down into an approximate uniformity in external appearance, though the inner development of individuals differed widely.

---

* *The Secret Doctrine*, vol. II, page 317.

VIII

THE "THIRD EYE"

AS the Monadic Ray illuminated by the light of the Higher Manas, like one prismatic ray of color blending with another and modifying it, associated itself more closely with the lower principles of the astral model-body, the passional-emotional principle of Kâma,* the vital solar energy of Prâna,* and the material molecular body, man lost many of the spiritual powers, while the intellectual ones — the rays of the Higher Manas — grew stronger. Even at the end of the Third Race man still possessed an organ of spiritual vision in activity. The Greek legend of the Kyklopes with an eye in the forehead was a recollection of this, for a Third Eye, the "Eye of S'iva," the organ of spiritual perception, was in full activity in Lemurian days.

* See Manual No. 2, *Seven Principles of Man*.

The mythological three Kyklopes, *the sons of Heaven and Earth,* symbolize the last three sub-races of the Third Root Race, and the legend of the famous hero Odysseus who put out the eye of Polyphemos, a Cyclopean giant, with a red-hot brand, is based upon the psycho-physiological atrophy of the Third Eye. The same legend with a few variations is found in Ireland, where Finn is said to have destroyed a wicked giant's eye with a heated *iron* spit. Iron is a symbol of passion and desire.

Civilization has ever developed the physical and intellectual at the cost of the psychic and spiritual. The command and the guidance over his own psychic nature, which foolish men now associate with the supernatural, were with early Humanity innate and congenital, and came to man as naturally as walking and thinking.*

With the " Fall " of man into material conditions, the Third Eye, the spiritual organ of vision, was gradually transformed (physically) into a simple gland, and ceased to perform its function in the vast majority of men. It is

---

* *The Secret Doctrine,* vol. II, page 318.

known as the Pineal gland or *Conarium*, and is deeply covered by the posterior part of the cerebral hemisphere. Certain saurians of the Secondary geological period possessed a well-defined third eye, and it is a singular fact that the most perfect known living representative of the reptiles with this organ developed, is an inhabitant of New Zealand, one of the surviving remnants of Lemuria. It is a small lizard, *Hatteria* (*Sphenodon*) *punctata*, which has a well-defined third eye with lens and optic nerve, under the skin of the top of the head. This eye may be sensitive to light, but is useless for distinct physical vision. The existing forms of life on Australia and New Zealand resemble those of the Secondary period more closely than those in any other part of the world.

While the Third Eye was in man, and still is when aroused by training, the organ of spiritual sight, (not ordinary astral clairvoyance, which requires no special purification) in the animal it was that of objective vision; having performed its function it was replaced in the course of physical evolution from the simple to the complex, by two eyes, and thus was stored and laid aside by Nature for further use in aeons to come. (H. P. Blavatsky)

The "War in Heaven" of Christian Theology is related — in one of its meanings — to the Third Race. H. P. Blavatsky says:

The Third Race was pre-eminently the bright shadow, at first, of the gods, whom tradition exiles on Earth after the allegorical war in Heaven; which became still more allegorical on Earth, for it was the war between spirit and matter. This war will last till the inner and divine man adjusts his outer terrestrial self to his own spiritual nature. Till then the dark and fierce passions of the former will be at eternal feud with his master, the Divine Man. But the *animal* will be tamed one day, because its nature will be changed, and harmony will reign once more between the two as before the "Fall," when even mortal man was *created* by the Elements and was not born.*

Physical changes in outer Nature accompanied the atrophy of the Third Eye and the development of the brain-mind; the climate,

* *The Secret Doctrine,* vol. II, page 268.

which had been pleasant and equable, altered, partly in consequence of changes in the direction of the Earth's axis.

The eternal spring became constant change and seasons succeeded. Cold forced man to build shelters and devise clothing. Then man appealed to the superior Fathers. . . . Divine Kings descended and taught men sciences and arts, for man could live no longer in the first land, which' had turned into a white frozen corpse.*

The first inhabited land upon which the earliest types of man appeared was around the North Pole, and during the Second Race this gradually extended. The Greeks preserved a tradition of this land of delight, calling it the Hyperborean region, the favorite abode of Apollo the God of light. Fossils of magnolias and other semi-tropical plants, lignite and coal seams are found in the strata now buried under the everlasting snows of the Arctic regions. These and the fossils brought back recently from the South Polar lands confirm some of the statements in *The Secret Doctrine*

---

* *The Secret Doctrine,* vol. II, page 201.

concerning the warm periods at both "ends" in various prehistoric ages. The climate of the habitable world at the commencement of the Third Race must have been almost perfect, but as man " fell " and the struggle between the higher and the lower commenced, the natural surroundings synchronously became less agreeable. The idea given in the Bible allegory that the animals " fell " under the curse with Adam, is founded upon the significant truth that man is the creator of his surroundings, and that Nature simply obeys the demands made upon her. As long as man is the sport of his passions, and crucifies the higher part of himself, the Christos within, Nature will produce the earthquakes, the storms, the extremes of heat and cold, and venomous and noxious animals will multiply. These things could not exist unless there was a cause for them, for " Nature exists for the soul's experience." * They are instruments which the law of Karma has developed for the discipline of sentient beings. They are the

* Patanjali's *Yoga Aphorisms.*

"curses coming home to roost," in a very literal sense. As H. P. Blavatsky says:

Intimately, or rather indissolubly, connected with Karma [the Law of Action and perfect Justice] then, is the law of rebirth, or of the reincarnation of the same spiritual individuality in a long, almost interminable, series of personalities. The latter are like the various costumes and characters played by the same actor, with each of which that actor identifies himself and is identified by the public, for the space of a few hours. . . . But the outer, visible character is supposed to be ignorant of the fact. In actual life that ignorance is, unfortunately, but too real. Nevertheless, the *permanent* individuality is fully aware of the fact, though, through the atrophy of the "spiritual" eye in the physical body, that knowledge is unable to impress itself on the consciousness of the false personality.*

---

* *The Secret Doctrine,* vol. II, page 306.

IX

RISE OF ATLANTIS

AFTER the Lemurians had existed for
ages as beings not very different from
the mankind of later times, yet more spiritual
than intellectual, a gradual division took place
into two well-marked sections, the Sons of
Light and the Sons of Darkness. Selfish desire increased and the decline of the Third
Race set in rapidly, but was not allowed to
proceed too far. The Law of Progress prevented too great a downfall by the destruction
of a large portion of the individuals through
the breaking up of the Lemurian Continent.
Simultaneously with the decay of the Third
Race civilizations, the beginnings of the new
type of man, the Fourth, began to appear, and
new lands arose from the sea to take the place
of the previous continent. Some of the islands
of Polynesia are remains of some of the moun-

tain tops of long-forgotten Lemuria, and the native traditions of a universal deluge, etc., greatly puzzled the early missionaries, who could not conceive how the ignorant savages, living in widely scattered islands, had obtained stories closely resembling those of the Creation and the Flood in the Bible. Australia and New Zealand are the largest parts of Lemuria now existing, but there are other portions, such as Ceylon, "Lanka," which is a remnant of a northern highland of Lemuro-Atlantis, and the Polar lands, though the latter belong properly to the First and Second continents.

Lemuria is said to have perished finally 700,000 years before the commencement of the Tertiary age of Geology. The highest group of its inhabitants, the comparatively few "Sons of Light," were not disturbed by the upheavals, for they had taken precautions and had moved away to safer regions; most of the small proportion of the average mankind that escaped centered towards land which is now under the waters of the north Atlantic.

They formed the nucleus of the next Root-Race, the Atlantean, and from that land the coming great Atlantean civilization spread over the new continent that was rising. Nature never breaks the continuity of her processes, so no hard and fast line can be drawn as to when one race ends and another begins. For many thousands of years the first sub-race of the Fourth had been developing parallel with the culminating of the last sub-races of the Third, just as we see today a new sub-race of our Fifth Root-Race forming in America; so that the relic of mankind saved from destruction contained representatives in all degrees of advancement.

The diagram following, taken from *The Secret Doctrine,* will make the scheme of human development during the Fourth Round a little clearer. It should be well remembered that it is not only mankind as a whole, but man as the individual Ego, whose progress we are tracing. The Races are the temporary vehicles of the larger life of the Egos constituting them, and though they may perish when

they have served their purpose, and before
they have fallen too deeply into degradation,
the immortal Ego simply passes on to the next
experience and will continue to do so until
the succeeding Manvantara, or World-Period.

EVOLUTION OF ROOT-RACES IN THE FOURTH
ROUND, ON " GLOBE " D.

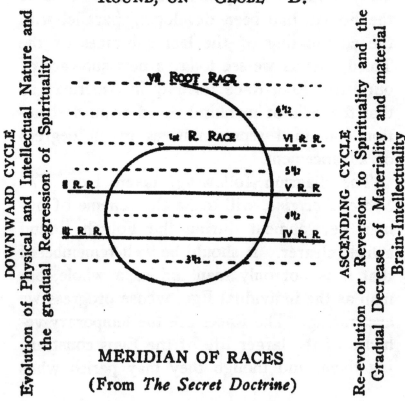

MERIDIAN OF RACES

(From *The Secret Doctrine*)

X

FALL OF ATLANTIS

FAR back in what we are accustomed to call antiquity, but which in true relationship to the ages of past human experience is but as yesterday, Plato, the Greek Initiate, revealed a glimpse of a surprising knowledge of the mysterious continent and civilization of Atlantis. His account is merely a sketch of the destruction of the last islands remaining after the greater catastrophes, for he was not permitted to give the full story of the lost antediluvian world, and of what he did give we have but a portion. But, fortunately, besides the legends in the Indian Purânas and elsewhere, which are difficult to interpret, there are other and more complete records in the possession of the Custodians of the Wisdom of the Ages, Theosophy; and it is from these that H. P. Blavatsky selected a few passages of importance to us in our study of the place of man in Nature.

It is not possible in these few pages to quote the geological, archaeological, and historical evidences as to the location and characteristics of the vanished continent of Atlantis. The student will find in *The Secret Doctrine* a mass of interesting evidence concerning it. The Indians of both Hemispheres, the Greeks, and other peoples, have handed down clear though partly allegorized accounts. Donnelly's *Atlantis* contains much — so far as *data* are concerned — that is valuable to students.

Atlantis gradually took form as Lemuria broke up under the turbulent disruptive forces of the adolescent period of Earth's growth, and as the portion of humanity which escaped the destruction spread afar, they peopled the newly risen lands and some of the old that were not submerged, with a race which subsequently touched the lowest depths of materiality that the world has seen. Since the Atlantean period man has been rising, though with many cyclic depressions, for the Atlantean civilization marked a turning-point in the history of the Earth. Until then mankind was *slowly descending into material conditions with a corresponding obscuration in spirituality.* The Atlanteans stand as the apotheosis of matter, and it was in those far-distant days that the heaviest Karma of the human race was generated, a Karma which is holding us back from the advance we should otherwise make, and whose existence explains many of the difficulties and anomalies of life. Humanity reached its fullest physical development in the Fourth Race, the physical bodies themselves being much larger than at present. The old saying that " there were giants in those days," was correct when applied to the Atlanteans. The curious decrease in the size of many organisms, which is so well marked in the case of the fearful saurians of the Secondary period — now represented by comparatively minute reptilian forms — also took place in the human kingdom; but as the practice of cremation was almost universal we are not likely to find many remains of gigantic human bones. Immense footprints have been found in the geologic strata of Nevada and Ohio, U. S. A., which seem to be human, but geology has not definitely sanctioned the claim that they are so. H. P. Blavatsky was very definite in her statements that undeniable proofs would be forthcoming, at the right time, of the conditions of life in the lost continent of Atlantis; so we can well afford to wait.

The Fourth Race started under far less favorable conditions than the Third, and towards its decline the story of Lemuria was repeated on lower levels; the same fight between the higher and lower natures within and without was waged, but more mercilessly; and as that was the age of Passion and Desire *in excelsis* and the eclipse of spirituality, the result was mainly in favor of the lower principles for a long time. But not for ever, for, although the majority of the Atlanteans were not the descendants of the higher group of the Third Race, the " one third that remained faithful " fought such a good fight that they were enabled to escape before the Deluge from the lands that had been cursed by the evil-doers, and to become the progenitors of the majority of our present, Aryan, humanity. The story of Noah's Deluge is, in one of its aspects, a fanciful account of the great Atlantean submersion; but it also has deeper meanings, one of which allegorizes the primeval building of the world.

Full *personal* responsibility came to the man of the Atlantean period, and although the last or final choice between spiritual advancement on the one side, and materialism or personal aggrandizement on the other, " good and evil," has not yet come for the mass of humanity, and will not until the next Round, a long step in that direction was taken by the Atlanteans. But Nature is merciful, and the world is not destined to perish ingloriously; so before the mischief had become irreparable, "the law that moves to righteousness" again arrested further degradation by giving a shock which allowed the Egos to start anew with a fresh opportunity, upon new lands not soaked through with the evil memories of past sins. The majority of the Atlantean evil-doers perished finally amid indescribable terrors, and the ocean soon obliterated all remains of that proud civilization which had misapplied greater powers than any with which we have since been entrusted. The last large destruction took place towards the close of the Meiocene age, when the Alps were upraised. Most of those then destroyed were of the giant race; but mankind was already diminishing in size, and when the final destruction of the few remaining islands upon which Atlanteans still existed took place, only about 11,000 years ago, men had long before assumed their present proportions. It was the latter destruction to which Plato refers when he handed on the tradition that the gods had caused the wicked Atlanteans to perish 9,000 years before his time. In *The Secret Doctrine** H. P. Blavatsky quotes, from an ancient esoteric commentary, a most thrilling description of the escape of the " faithful " and of the struggle which

* *The Secret Doctrine*, vol. ii, page 427.

took place between the Sons of Darkness and
the Sons of Light just before the final break-
up of one of the largest island regions of Atlantis. Air-ships of great perfection were used
by the " White Adepts," and the measures tak-
en and the weapons spoken of illustrate a
much deeper knowledge of natural forces —
magic — than science has yet suspected, fortunately for us in this age of selfishness!

As may be seen by a reference to the diagram on page 54 the fifth or Aryan race had
started some time before the last destruction
of Atlantis. Descended from the more spiritualized and better class of Atlanteans, a few
had preserved the knowledge of their ancestors and were ready to revive it when the
race demanded it. The institution of the
Mysteries in all countries at a later period was
an effort, and fortunately a successful one, to
preserve the ancient wisdom from the profan-
ation it had suffered in Atlantis. An example
of the profound knowledge of the Atlanteans
is shown in the astronomical computations of
Indian astronomy, which are based upon a

little that was permitted to escape from the guardianship of the Mysteries.

It was in Atlantis, too, that language took its inflectional form, after having passed from the stage of musical nature-sounds in the Second Race, to monosyllabic speech in the later Third, and then to the agglutinative form in the Fourth. Of course writing was well known to the Fourth Race, for during its long career it possessed civilizations higher than were those of Greece or Rome in their palmiest days, and even far higher than our own civilization today, though it may have been lost to the world at large during the period of confusion when the first sub-races of the Fifth were forming. The traces of writing in the " Stone Age " (which belongs to our epoch) are not conclusive; and yet it is strange and entirely unexplained by modern science, that Palaeolithic man could draw animals upon antlers and cavern walls, etc., in a style that would not disgrace a good draughtsman of today, and which is certainly superior in accuracy to that of some of the

REINDEER ENGRAVED ON ANTLER BY PALAEOLITHIC MAN. (*After Geikie*)

Egyptian conventional representations of animals, or to the crude drawings of the famous Bayeux tapestry which was woven perhaps five hundred thousand years after the time of the supposed brutal "primitive" man — a savage that we are told was nearly on a level with his hypothetical ape-grandfather! Palaeolithic (ancient Stone Age) man was in reality carrying on some memories of the perished civilizations, as his artistic talent shows; the Neolithic (new Stone Age) man who followed him had lost this power, although he was improving in some other respects. The Palaeolithic drawings show no resemblance to the scrawls of children, but display concentrated observation and high technical skill — in other words, qualities of advanced civilization!

With this gradual break-up of the Fourth Race civilizations, which were varied and numerous, the dawn of what is known *to science* as the human period, begins. In actual years the distance is enormous from the first subrace of the Fifth Race to the present day, and what is generally supposed to be the whole history of man " does not go back," as H. P. Blavatsky says, " further than the fantastic origins of our fifth sub-race, a ' few thousands ' of years." In the brief space at our disposal, only the most cursory reference can be made to the progress of humanity during the Fifth Race.

The destruction of the spiritually degraded Atlanteans gave a shock to the survivors which resulted in the sinking of material civilization for a long time over the *main portion* of the globe; we are not yet told exactly what proportion of the world kept some vestiges of the past greatness, but it cannot have been large. Anyway, the effect of the fresh start was good, for it provided conditions under which the later comparatively unsophisticated tribes could be helped by advanced souls who incarnated among them and taught them the elements of the arts and sciences. In every tradition that has come down to us from antiquity a Golden Age is spoken of — the " Garden of Eden " in the Bible — and, although in some cases this unmistakably refers to the

First, Second, and the early Third Races, when rudimentary mankind had not fallen into materiality, it may generally be taken to mean the Dawn of the Fifth when mankind was again comparatively pure and happy, and was guided by semi-divine kings, Adepts of wisdom and compassion. In Egypt the traditions of many dynasties of gods and heroes were recorded by Manetho, and have actually come down to us, though the lists of names have been mutilated. While no doubt the details of the Greek, Hindû, Egyptian, Central American and Scandinavian cosmogonies and primitive histories of mankind are largely allegorical, their *general* agreement is not due to chance. Those who have given Theosophy to the world possess definite information that there was a time of spiritual brightness before ordinary history begins, and that it could truly be called a Golden Age. By degrees the same old process of materializing came into action; and as the " family " races, or smaller divisions of the sub-races, differentiated into the nations of the later ages, we arrive at " historic " and present times, with the numerous red, yellow, brown, black, and white representatives of the complex developments of the great evolutionary process of human expansion. Although we have descended into an age of moral and spiritual darkness (not intellectual), as compared with the Golden Ages it must not be forgotten that in the great journey of the soul from spiritual conditions through the material and back to a higher point, it is subject to a continual series of smaller cyclic ups and downs, and that even in the darkest time necessary experience is being gained. As we have long since passed the densest materiality of the Fourth Race, every step onwards is leading to higher conditions, and although the Road seems to cross many a hill and descend into dark valleys, its general tendency is upwards all the time.

XI

ORIGIN OF RELIGIONS

ONE of the most interesting points in the development of man as a soul is the growth of religions. The early Races, the First and Second, not being deeply immersed in matter nor endowed with mind and responsibility, had no need for the help of any form of religion such as we understand; they lived in harmony with Nature, and of the later period H. P. Blavatsky says:

At the dawn of his consciousness, the man of the Third Root Race had thus no beliefs that could be called *religion*. That is to say, he was equally as ignorant of "gay religions, full of pomp and gold" as of any system of faith or outward worship. But if the term is to be defined as the binding together of the masses in one form of reverence paid to those we feel higher than ourselves, of piety — as a feeling expressed by a child toward a loved parent — then even the earliest Lemurians had a religion —

and a most beautiful one — from the very beginning of their intellectual life. . . . It was the " Golden Age " in those days of old, the age when the "gods walked the earth, and mixed freely with the mortals." . . . It was the Atlanteans, the first progeny of *semi-divine* man after his separation into sexes — hence the first-begotten aad humanly-born mortals — who became the first " Sacrificers " to the *god of matter.* They stand in the far-away dim past, in ages more than prehistoric, as the . . . first anthropomorphists who worshiped form and matter. That worship degenerated very soon into *self-worship,* thence led to phallicism, or that which reigns supreme to this day in the symbolisms of every exoteric religion of ritual, dogma, and form.*

But, as the writer of *The Secret Doctrine* says elsewhere,

A phallic worship has developed only with the gradual loss of the keys to the inner meanings of religious symbols,

and there was a day when religions were pure. After the destruction of Atlantis, a few wise guides who carried on the knowledge of the past and reincarnated time after time for the helping of the new child-race, brought out the

---

* *The Secret Doctrine,* vol. II, pages 272-3.

facts as to man's real nature and his relationship to his (inner) God, in symbolic ceremony and definite illustration in the teaching of the Mysteries. The Aryan Hindûs, whose ancestors were among the early descendants of the first sub-race of the Fifth, have preserved in their Scriptures the clearest records of the primitive wisdom; but after all, even these are so bewilderingly confused and full of "blinds," for which the key has been lost (for the public) that they are all but a sealed book to modern readers, *not excepting* the learned Sanskritists of the Western Universities. But the last quarter of the Nineteenth century, the period when Materialism was attempting to crush the belief in anything spiritual, was chosen by Those who are watching every movement of human thought and action and who are the Guardians of the primeval Wisdom-Religion, Theosophy, in its purity, to give out a few facts showing that there was a primitive KNOWLEDGE, and that all modern systems of religion are modifications, perversions, or merely fractions of it. Although that which has been given out is only a glimpse, it has placed students in such a position that when the time ripens they will be prepared to receive fuller light.

This idea of there being truth and real *knowledge* in the earliest forms of religion is new to the scientific investigator. The favorite hypothesis of the day (putting aside the crude literal interpretation of the biblical Genesis, which has been abandoned by nearly everyone capable of understanding the value of evidence) is that every religious concept can be traced back to absurd myths of primitive savages living a few thousand years ago; and that modern savages provide perfect illustrations of the state of primitive man in religious views as well as in their intellectual development, and that — given sufficient time — the savage races would develop civilizations of a high order, and religions as good as those of today.

Theosophists have always contended that this hypothesis is not in accord with the facts. The lowest savages are mostly decaying relics of the lost Lemuro-Atlantean or Atlantean sub-races. This does not mean that all the *individuals* composing them are going down hill — quite the contrary. The reincarnating Egos in such miserable vestiges as the Veddahs of Ceylon, the lower African tribes, etc., have only come into Fourth Round terrestrial incarnation comparatively lately, and have not got to face the heaped-up bad Karma that the superior races have still to face owing to their mistakes in the past. The door of incarnation into humanity closed at the midway point of the Rounds, and the last Monad incarnated in human form before the beginning of the Fifth Race, with only one exception — the *anthropoid ape,* which is really a degraded man-animal, and which will have its opportunity of gaining complete manhood in the next Round.

XII

MAN AND THE ANTHROPOID APES

TURNING for a moment to the question of the origin of the anthropoid apes — the gorilla, chimpanzee, orang-utang, and gibbon — the fundamental distinction between the attitude of Theosophy and that of Materialism is well marked. Instead of being a mere animal with a highly developed brain " secreting mind or thought," * — the soul thus being a simple function of matter, a by-product, perishing at death like music when the harp is broken — Theosophy teaches that the real man is a " fallen god," a self-conscious being who has been immortal in the past as he will be in the future. The Monads of many of the animal races which strongly resemble man in bodily structure, possess *the potentialities* of the highest development, but these are still

* " No phosphorus, no thought," Moleschott.

latent, for they have not been awakened by
the incarnation of the spark of godlike Mind.
The possession of the higher Self-conscious-
ness, though as yet in truth in a very incomplete degree, *is what makes man a man.* To
derive human conscience and human intellect
from the brain-faculties or instinctual mind of
animals by Natural Selection, Survival of the
Fittest, etc., as the only causes thereof, would
be as hopeless a problem as to make a per-
petual motion machine, for something cannot
be produced from nothing. The animal Monads are getting necessary experience in physical life, and in some future age the divine
Mind-Egos now incarnated in our human
forms will *project the spark to arouse the*
latent fires in the lower lives; then those ani-
mal-Monads will have become human-Monads.
H. P. Blavatsky spoke in severe condemnation
of the belittling of human nature with its
essentially divine attributes (however degraded
and obscured) by modern speculation, which
tries to reduce the activity of the mighty and
awe-inspiring divine Ego overshadowing each

human being, the wonderful and mysterious reincarnating Self, to a mere function of the brain of a creature supposed to be but the advanced product of a hairy quadrumanous ancestor.

What, then, is the origin of the anthropoid apes? H. P. Blavatsky calls them a " bastard branch grafted on the original stock " of humanity. The " common ancestor " of man and the anthropoids was — *man himself,* in a far distant age. In the Third *Round* (not Race), the human Monad, in building around itself changeful and varying forms of an ethereal and ephemeral nature, at one period adopted that of an ape-*like* form (but it was not an ape, but *man — there were no apes then*), a form which was copied and humanized for man's habitation again in the denser conditions of the earlier part of the Third *Race* of the *Fourth Round;* for each Round in the *descending* order repeats the previous experience, but in more material substance. This was before the full descent of the Mânasaputras, the Higher Egos; and this early race of

the Third Round as it " fell into generation "
and separated into sexes, threw off many imperfect offshoots, some of which, mating with
certain animals, produced forms which ultimately modified (in the Tertiary geological
period) into the ancestors of the anthropoids
of our day. This act was repeated by some of
the later degraded Atlanteans in full consciousness of the wrong. Resulting from this bestiality of early man, there were so many degrees of half-human animals at that dim and
distant period, that we may fully expect to
find fossilized remains of their descendants
as "missing-links" even more anthropoid in
character than the thigh-bone and skull-frag-
ment found in Java a few years ago, about
which so much has been said. Java happens
to be a portion of Lemuria, and a probable
place to find such remains; but H. P. Blavatsky says that

In order to prove the Huxley-Haeckelian theories
of the descent of man, it is not *one*, but a great
number of *"missing links"* — a true ladder of progressive evolutionary steps — that would have to be

first found and then presented by Science to thinking and reasoning humanity before it would abandon
belief in gods and the immortal Soul for the worship of Quadrumanic ancestors.*

A remarkable corroboration of the early
connexion between humanity and the four
species of anthropoids mentioned above, which
are said in the Esoteric Philosophy to owe
their origin *to man*, has been discovered recently in certain tests of their blood. The
injection of a serum proved that the blood of
the four anthropoids reacted in the same manner as human blood, while that of other mon-
keys behaved differently under the same tests.

Another significant observation supporting
the Theosophical teaching that man is not derived from an animal ancestry, is that an *in-
verse order* exists in the brain of the anthropoid apes when compared with man. In the
apes the middle convolutions of the brain appear before those of the frontal lobe (the latter supposed to be the instrument of the higher
mental activities), but in man the frontal con-

---

* *The Secret Doctrine*, vol. II, page 661.

volutions are formed first. As the anthropoids are the descendants of man and some extinct species of mammals which lived in the Meiocene age, and as the animal side is still predominant in them, the development of the brain in the above order is what might be expected from the Theosophical standpoint. Two or three years ago a fossil jaw of an extinct kind of chimpanzee was discovered in North-Western India, having characteristics far more human than the present representatives possess, showing that there has been no advance towards the human type.

Then again, the writer of *The Secret Doctrine* says, speaking of man:

His intellect develops and increases with age, while his facial bones and jaws diminish and straighten, thus being more and more spiritualized: whereas with the ape it is the reverse. In its youth the anthropoid is far more intelligent and good-natured, while with age it becomes duller; and, as its skull recedes and seems to diminish as it grows, its facial bones and jaws develop, the brain being finally crushed, and thrown entirely back, to make with every day more room for the animal type. The organ of thought — the brain — recedes and diminishes, entirely conquered and replaced by that of the wild beast — the jaw apparatus. . . .   Owing to the very type of his development man *cannot descend* from either an ape or an ancestor common to both, but shows his origin from a type far superior to himself. . . .   On the other hand, the pithecoids, the orang-outang, the gorilla, and the chimpanzee *can,* and, as the Occult Sciences teach, *do,* descend from the animalized Fourth human Root-Race, being the product of man and an extinct species of mammal — whose *remote* ancestors were themselves the product of Lemurian bestiality — which lived in the Meiocene age.*

Much more might be said upon this crucial subject but for exigencies of space. The student will find the subject very fully treated in *The Secret Doctrine.*

* *The Secret Doctrine,* vol. II, pages 682-3.

XIII

THE FUTURE OF HUMANITY

RETURNING to the question of the origin of religions, evidences for the statement that the principal religions of our times were derived from one common source at the beginning of the Fifth Race, when the separation of the Âryan (using the term *Âryan* in the technical Theosophical sense) families began, are found in the wonderful resemblances between them. For instance it is well known that the accounts of the Creation and the Flood, the cycle of the story of Jesus and many an event of his career, can be more or less closely paralleled in a dozen other faiths; the doctrine of Trinity in Unity is as old as the hills; and the ethical teachings of the Sermon on the Mount are found as the moral basis of religions " from China to Peru." The allegorical stories upon which the forms of reli-

gion are based can be traced back into the
night of Time, and, according to the records
of the Custodians of the ancient Wisdom
(Theosophy) they were first of all produced
by Initiates to contain the truth in a form
capable of being understood to some extent
by the ordinary mind. Those properly qualified were taught *the deeper meanings.*

These forms of faith were gradually cor-
rupted, until it became necessary to re-state
the same truths in slightly modified fashion
for the better comprehension of the newly-
rising nations. It would be preposterous to
suppose primitive savages capable of inventing
myths containing the profound wisdom which
is hidden just beneath the surface of the sacred
beliefs. As if to prove the knowledge of their
framers, most of the world-scriptures contain
distinct allusions to the Rounds and Races
with their destructions and regenerations, and
in some cases so clearly that they can easily
be traced by anyone who holds the clue given
by Theosophy.

The positive teachings of Theosophy concerning the origins of mankind and of religion show that the "primitive savage" and "animistic" hypotheses are erroneous and incomplete, quite apart from their materializing tendency. These theories recognize nothing but the lower mind, the egotistic brain-personality, and the animal instincts. In trying to trace the development of man and the origins of the higher attributes of the soul, scientific Anthropology is blocked by its disregard of the Reincarnating Ego, the Higher Mind or *Manas,* of which the lower is but the shadow or emanation, hardly to be separated from the animal nature. Scientific writers — apparently laboring under the hypnotic weight of the famous date of 4004 B. C., the theological date of the "creation" — have also erred in limiting the duration of the human period to a few thousands of years, and in not recognizing the existence of the pre-historic civilizations. The presence of advanced Egos from previous manvantaras guiding the race at all times is unknown to them even as a theory. The only "primitive man" deserving the title was the rudimentary or incomplete "man" of the earlier Rounds and also of the pre-Lemurian age. He was very different from the " Stone-Age " type, who was a true man, even if degraded. That religion is a simple brain-mind production derived from observation of the natural phenomena of the Seasons, the Weather, etc., and that belief in the existence of the soul came from the childish imagination of savage men that dreams are real experiences, are suggestions which materialistic bias has rendered plausible to the scientific spirit of the age, which still suffers unconsciously to itself from the strong reaction against the irrational dogmas of scholastic theology. Scientific research has done excellent service in freeing millions from degrading servitude to the tyranny of bigoted ecclesiasticism and superstition, but when it tries to prove that there is no spiritual foundation for religion, and that man, in seeing a divine consciousness at work in himself and in Nature has been the dupe of his imagination, it is time to call a halt. The materialistic theory of the origin of the religious faiths cannot permanently satisfy the bulk of mankind, whether cultivated or otherwise, for there is a deep-seated conviction that there must be something more in them than mere convenient illusions founded on ignorance and folly and built up by fraud.

The strength of the materialistic position, such as it is, has lain principally in the absence of any reasonable explanation of such extraordinary allegories as those of *Genesis, Ezekiel,* or the *Apocalypse,* in the *Bible;* of the Chaldaean legends; of the Hindû *Vedas* and *Purânas;* of the Egyptian *Book of the Dead;* of the poems of Hesiod in Greece; of the Central American *Popol Vuh;* of the Scandinavian epics, and the rest. The keys have at last been furnished by Theosophy. The Sacred books of the different races and religions were inspired by the *initiated Teachers* of former days, "Sons" of one common Mother-System, so it is not wonderful that these writings and traditions even today can reveal their meaning to him who has the key.

It is a long lane that has no turning, and it is worthy of note that an uneasiness is growing in high intellectual quarters as to the accuracy of the orthodox scientific theory of religious evolution, and that an interpretation more in harmony with Theosophical teaching has been forced upon at least one scientific man of the first rank by the stern logic of facts. Professor Sir W. M. Ramsay * expresses the popular theory as follows:

The modern method is based on the assumption that there takes place normally a continuous development in religion, in thought, and in civilization, since primitive times; that such a development has been practically universal among the more civilized races; that as to certain less civilized races either they have remained stationary, or progress among them has been abnormally slow; that the primitive religion is barbarous, savage, bloodthirsty, and low in the scale of civilization, and that the line of growth normally is toward the milder, the more gracious and the nobler forms of religion; that the primitive types of religion can be recovered by studying the savage of the present day, and that the lowest savage is the most primitive.

* *Contemporary Review*, 1907, London.

Instead of finding that a dispassionate examination of the facts supports this position, the Professor says the reverse is the case:

Wherever evidence exists, with the rarest exceptions, the history of religion among men is a history of degeneration; and the development of a few Western nations in inventions and in civilization during recent centuries should not blind us to the fact that among the vast majority of nations the history of manners and civilization is a story of degeneration. Wherever you find a religion that grows purer and loftier, you find the prophet, the thinker, the teacher, who is in sympathy with the Divine, and he tells you he is speaking the message of God, not his own message. Are these prophets all impostors and deceivers? or do they speak the truth, and need only to have their words rightly, *i. e*. sympathetically understood? . . . The primitive savage, who develops naturally out of the stage of Totemism into the wisdom of Sophocles and Socrates . . . is unknown to me. I find nothing even remotely resembling him in the savages of modern times. . . . I was forced by the evidence to the view that degeneration is the outstanding fact in religious history and that the modern theory often takes the last products of degeneration as the facts of primitive religion.

Space will not permit further quotation of similar passages which express more or less closely what Theosophists have been teaching for more than a quarter of a century past, in face of the strongest opposition from materialism and conventional orthodoxy. The " prophet, the thinker, the teacher," referred to above, " who is in sympathy with the Divine," reminds us of the Theosophical teaching that there have always been such advanced souls in the van of progress, giving mankind the exact kind of spiritual food it could assimilate at the time, and also protecting it from the evils that constantly threaten it. These advanced souls have never been absent; they are not wanting today, although not known to the world. The modern savage is the flotsam and jetsam of past greatness; and our civilized races that now pride themselves upon their high culture, will, when their race is run, vegetate, degenerate, and die out in future ages, like the natives of Tasmania have in our time, for this is the law. The Egos now inhabiting the bodies of the most advanced races will not, of course, remain in the lower human forms except in cases of persistent evil-living lasting from incarnation to incarnation, but will pass into the new and more perfect races which are beginning already to show faint signs of appearing. Less advanced Egos will take up the forms of the present mankind. *The Secret Doctrine* says:

The Americans have become in only three centuries a "primary race" *pro tem.*, before becoming a race apart. . . . They are, in short, the germs of the *Sixth* sub-race, and in some few hundred years more will become most decidedly the pioneers of that race which must succeed to the present European or fifth sub-race, in all its new characteristics. After this, in about 25,000 years, they will launch into preparations for the seventh sub-race; until . . . the Sixth Root-Race will have appeared on the stage of our Round. . . . The Fifth will overlap the Sixth Race for many hundreds of millenniums, changing with it slower than its new successor, still changing in stature, general physique, and mentality, just as the Fourth overlapped our Aryan Race, and the Third had overlapped the Atlanteans.

This process of preparation for the Sixth great Race must last throughout the whole sixth and seventh sub-races. But the *last* remnants of the Fifth Continent will not disappear until some time after the birth of the *new* Race. . . . Mankind will not grow again into giant bodies as in the case of the Lemurians and the Atlanteans; because while the evolution of the Fourth race led the latter down to the very bottom of materiality in its physical development, the present Race is on its ascending arc; and the Sixth will be rapidly growing out of its bonds of matter, and even of flesh.*

As in the earlier Rounds the Monad was assimilating the various principles in very shadowy and ethereal vehicles; and as in this Round the Desire-principle is dominant; so in the next (Fifth) Round, fully developed Reason, the Higher Mânasic principle in each man, must fully conquer the passional nature or the great pilgrimage will have been in vain, and it will have to return to the crucible of existence to start afresh at some future time. The *Mahâtmâ* is one who has pushed so far ahead of the obstacles that impede the average man that he may justly be called a " Sixth-Round " being, one who has safely passed be-

---

* *The Secret Doctrine,* vol. II, page 444.

yond that supreme danger point which will meet humanity as a whole during the Fifth Round, called the final "moment of choice." This critical period has to be faced, but it will only prove fatal to that portion of mankind which persists in the egotism of personal self-ishness. An individual may lose the bliss of one or more Devachanic interludes, the heavenly states between one life on earth and another, by a mis-spent life, for the reason that there is nothing in that life to provide material for the Devachanic experiences; but the Law is just beyond human understanding, and as there are many lives in which to remedy past errors, the great majority of the race will pass on in safety to a transcendentally glorious future. "Eye hath not seen, nor ear heard, neither have entered into the heart of man, the things which God hath prepared for them that love him."

But the preparation for this great end must be ceaseless struggle against the passional nature now so strongly entrenched within us, and Those who really belong to the Fifth and

Sixth Rounds, who are Wisdom and Compassion embodied, are working with the Divine Law and giving continual though unseen help to their brothers, the other struggling fragments of humanity making their way up the weary hill of life. Mankind is not left to wander too far from the road to safety. The " sense of separatenesss," of personal selfish isolation and indifference to the welfare of the rest of humanity, our " other selves," is the only heresy recognized in Theosophy, but it is a deadly one and indeed prevalent; the spread of true knowledge and practice of brotherhood is the only remedy. To do this effectually, which is the object that all the great Teachers of humanity have lived for, was the aim in starting the Theosophical Society to meet and guide the conditions of the New Order of the Ages. This Movement, established on unsectarian lines, and supported by Those who have real *knowledge* — not mere inference — of the history of the past and of man's real nature, is a unique phenomenon in modern times. The opportunity offered to men by THE UNIVERSAL BROTHERHOOD AND THEOSOPHICAL SOCIETY for serving humanity with the greatest efficiency and conservation of energy, and through this personal service to obtain the high impersonal reward of realizing the existence of an inner communion with the real Self, the Higher, Immortal Ego, the only reward the true Theosophist desires, is the greatest that mankind has had for many ages.

THE SOUL
The stars shall fade away, the Sun himself
Grow dim with age, and Nature sink in years,
But thou shalt flourish in immortal youth,
Unhurt amid the war of elements,
The wreck of matter, and the crash of worlds.
ADDISON

There is no Religion Higher than Truth

The
Universal Brotherhood
and
Theosophical Society

Established for the benefit of the people of the earth & all creatures

OBJECTS

This BROTHERHOOD is part of a great and universal movement which has been active in all ages.

This Organization declares that Brotherhood is a fact. Its principal purpose is to teach Brotherhood, demonstrate that it is a fact in nature and make it a living power in the life of humanity.

Its subsidiary purpose is to study ancient and modern religions, science, philosophy and art; to investigate the laws of nature and the divine powers in man.

*   *   *

THE UNIVERSAL BROTHERHOOD AND THEOSOPHICAL SOCIETY, founded by H. P. Blavatsky at New York, 1875, continued after her death under the leadership of the co-founder, William Q. Judge, and now under the leadership of their successor, Katherine Tingley, has its Headquarters at the International Theosophical Center, Point Loma, California.

This Organization is not in any way connected with nor does it endorse any other societies using the name of Theosophy.